PATTERNED BACKGROUNDS FOR NEEDLEPOINT

Sheila Nassberg Marton/Muriel Brandwein Selick

VAN NOSTRAND REINHOLD COMPANY
New York   Cincinnati   Toronto   London   Melbourne

To David Alan Selick
who made possible the impossible

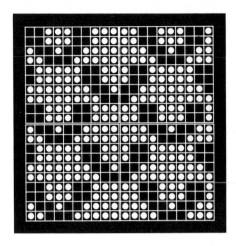

Printed in the United States of America
David Selick, Technical Consultant
Photographs by David Selick unless otherwise credited
Designed by Loudan Enterprise

Published in 1977 by Van Nostrand Reinhold Company
A division of Litton Educational Publishing, Inc.
450 West 33rd Street, New York, NY 10001, U.S.A.

Van Nostrand Reinhold Limited
1410 Birchmount Road, Scarborough, Ontario M1P 2E7,
Canada

Van Nostrand Reinhold Australia Pty. Limited
17 Queen Street, Mitcham, Victoria 3132, Australia

Van Nostrand Reinhold Company Limited
Molly Millars Lane, Workingham, Berkshire, England

16 15 14 13 12 11 10 9 8 7 6 5 4 3 2 1

Library of Congress Cataloging in Publication Data

Marton, Sheila Nassberg.
   Patterned backgrounds for needlepoint.

   Includes index.
   1. Canvas embroidery—Patterns.   I. Selick, Muriel
Brandwein, joint author.   II. Title.
TT778.C3M44   746.4'4   77-3147
ISBN 0-442-27480-7

ACKNOWLEDGMENTS

Many thanks to the following friends, for stitching some of the finished projects: Irene Marton
(12 years old), Willa Trestman, Gerri Kurzman,
Barbara Weber, Ronnie Malasky, Matthew
Selick (8 years old), with a little help from Steven
Selick (6 years old), and Frederic Marton (at 7½
years of age). All other work was designed and
stitched by the authors.

   We also want to thank Harriet and Robert
Cohen and Ellen and Richard T. Nassberg, for
permission to reproduce articles from their
collections; David Selick, Stuart Marton, and
Richard T. Nassberg, for their photographs; and
C. Audrey Bell, Robert S. Bramson, Richard T.
Nassberg, Dora Steinglass, and the staff of
Tenafly Public Library, Tenafly, New Jersey; for
all their help.

   Special thanks to our families, Herbert, Stuart,
Irene, and Frederic Marton and David, William,
Matthew, and Steven Selick, for their involve-
ment, which has given us unflagging support,
and to Mindy, whose enthusiasm for needlework provided the initial inspiration.

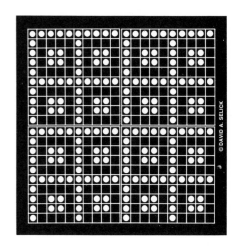

CONTENTS

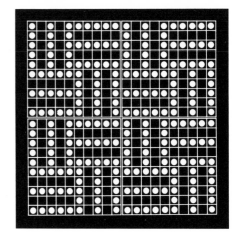

PREFACE

The idea of writing this book crystallized one Saturday evening at a dinner party. For a good number of years prior to that evening the two of us had run back and forth to each other's houses with ideas, had conferred over the telephone, had made pilgrimages in search of specific materials. We learned how to raise direct questions and, far more difficult, to answer with specific, candid suggestions.

We had initially used patterned backgrounds solely to break up the monotony of the solid, plain field—until we realized that they also provided additional areas for creativity and for implementing ideas, the chance to further embellish a canvas and enhance a design. Patterned backgrounds enabled us to individualize each work in a very personal and specific way. Before the evening ended, we had realized that the idea that was so exciting to us might well prove to be as intriguing and stimulating to others.

Most needlepoint today does not even consider designed backgrounds. We believe that most should. To be iconoclastic was not what either of us had in mind—what is more traditional than the millefleurs design? Each of us had seen the opportunity to enhance and to individualize every one of our canvases, to give each a unique quality unto itself. Each background offers the chance to complement the design in the center, enabling all the components to form a harmonious total design.

S.N.M.
M.B.S.

4

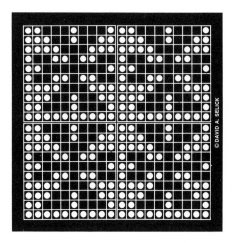
©DAVID A. SELICK

INTRODUCTION

Background takes up the major portion of most needlepoint canvases and the majority of work and time involved in their creation. In fact, eternity is defined by needlepointers as background! Working this area in one color and one stitch is tedious, slow, and uninspiring. Row after row of space filler offers little reward to your creativity and individuality. Canvases are generally worked from the center outward. Enthusiasm dwindles markedly as the embroiderer completes the focal design and proceeds to stitch the plain surrounding area. Design can break the monotony of the plain background. Until now background has received little or no attention in terms of the design or mood of the finished product's overall theme. Needlepoint is delightful; plain backgrounds are dull and tiresome.

One of the nation's most famous jewelry stores has display windows that draw awesome throngs. Each window shows one or two magnificent gems or pieces of jewelry. These pieces are never placed against a barren field: each window has a background, which acts as a backdrop and echoes or contrasts with the central figure. The viewer gets a total picture that evokes unity and balance of composition. Across the street another store displaying equally beautiful and precious gems by themselves attracts only a few people.

Needlework should be as much a combined endeavor as these famous windows, a fine watercolor, or an oil painting. All parts of the design should be joined into a whole, a work of art. Composition is produced by the selective use of proper color, size, form, and shape. Foreground and background should be planned in such a manner that each enhances the other. They are two distinct aspects, each equally important and equally dependent upon the other to provide the harmony and balance of the total composition. Background should enrich the canvas, give the central figure an appropriate setting, and establish the desired mood. Your personal mark should be apparent in each canvas: each should be individual, different from all others; each should contain a background adapted to the foreground and to the craftsman or recipient in a unique manner. Your work need not be repeated ad infinitum: it can become one-of-a-kind.

Whether you design your own creation or buy a kit, you can easily incorporate a patterned background in order to individualize the canvas. Once you can do any one of the three basic tent stitches (basketweave, continental, or half-cross), you can stitch any background pattern at your level of expertise. You need only select a background that will flatter the central figure and set the tone. The shape of the central object can also be reinforced in the background pattern. You can augment your own designs or personalize a commercial canvas. Your work need not be a copy but will be an original: imagination will lift it above those of others, giving you a source of continuing pride.

Patterned backgrounds bring excitement to the craftsman, to the finished work, and to those who see it. Patterned backgrounds make needlepoint a more creative endeavor. They help to avoid the eternity of stitching a plain field and the unnecessary monotony of working a solid, uninteresting expanse. The gratification of doing needlepoint is twofold: both the actual handwork and the handiwork itself.

This book has over two hundred of the limitless possibilities for backgrounds. The manifold ways in which you can give your canvas the mark of individuality and of your own craftsmanship will become apparent. Select a central design; incorporate an appropriate pattern for the background. These two simple steps will give additional meaning to your project. Designed backgrounds enrich neutral colors; they coordinate eclectic decors as well as shapes or the central theme. You will soon delight in creativity that can range as far as your imagination allows. You will take pride in the artistry that distinguishes your craftsmanship from the workmanship of others.

This book is written with the full scope of needlepoint buffs in mind, from the novice with kit in hand to the designer with paintbrush in hand. It has been a labor of love for us; we hope that it will inspire new enthusiasm for you. If patterned backgrounds are contagious, beware, for we have the bug.

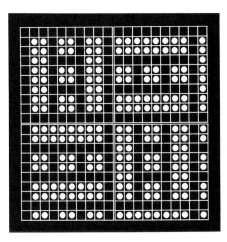

HOW TO BEGIN

This book is divided into several sections for your convenience and to provide a step-by-step introduction to the exciting field of creative and individual design. Customize your canvas; advance from novice-workman to artist-craftsman. This book includes basics such as kits, color, and project ideas.

The greatest portion of *Patterned Backgrounds For Needlepoint* is just that: patterned backgrounds. There are patterns to meet various tastes, styles, and themes. Each design is represented by a graph. Stitched examples of some patterns follow the graph section. Each classification is represented by three samples. Look at them along with their graphed counterparts in order to envision the subtle transition from graphed to stitched patterns. Illustrations of variations are included, combinations are explained, multiple ways of seeing and using each design are explored. The next section consists of color reproductions of finished works. Each project is numbered and cross-referenced with the appropriate graph; stitching techniques used are described. Variations of the graphed designs are noted.

Background designs consist of a pattern on a field: the two comprise the total background. In this book each background contains two colors, one for each element. To clarify the two elements, two shapes, a square and a circle, are used in each graph. Either shape can represent either the pattern or the field. In each graph at least one full repeat is represented, both horizontally and vertically. The scale is ten boxes to the inch (2.54 cm). Each box represents the intersection of a horizontal and a vertical thread on the canvas. Slightly wider lines divide the graph into equal sections of ten to facilitate counting stitches.

The designs are classified and numbered for your convenience. Each design and variation is named for its predominating element, such as stripes or diagonals, although many consist of several components. Each section—A, B, C, and D—contains several design categories, a full range of possibilities. Squint as you view the graphs in order to get the full impact of the designs. Each can be read in many ways:

1. hold book upright
2. hold book upside down
3. hold book sideways
4. enlarge or reduce pattern
5. change proportion
6. reverse squares and circles

The repeats of the design can be spaced:

1. vertically
2. horizontally
3. diagonally
4. closer together or further apart

Repeat the squares first and fill in the circles later or vice versa.

Variations can be produced by altering the original designs in many ways. Design elements can be combined to produce new patterns. Increasing the gauge will make the pattern bolder, but direction, scale, and style must

7

always be compatible. An initial may be introduced into or found in a design. A *J*, for example, may be seen as a series of hooked lines, an adaptation of a Greek key, or an Oriental lattice. If it is run on an angle, it may be seen as a diagonal design. You also can reverse the pattern and the field by focusing on the form of the field rather than on that of the pattern. Each person sees the design according to his own frame of reference.

The graphs are arranged in sections according to the complexity of the designs and upon the dexterity required to reproduce each pattern. The stitch count is also considered. These classifications are based upon our experience and upon that of students at every level of expertise. They are suggestions only: they are not irrevocable. Specific designs may be easier for some people than for others. A great deal of individuality is involved in reading and in stitching the graphs.

Select a pattern that falls within the scope of your own ability. Its style should coordinate with that of your central design; its shape should be compatible with that of the motif; its colors should harmonize with the central colors. The scale can be used as shown in the graph or altered to suit the proportions of the central design. Horizontal and vertical repeats are the easiest to accomplish. Diagonal repeats are more difficult: proper spacing can be tricky. Repeat your design horizontally and vertically in parallel panels. The repeats must always be exact. Clean-cut background designs are easiest to transfer: they will not conflict with the central motif. A fine composition will emerge in which none of the elements competes. Basic designs can suit the beginner as well as the accomplished embroiderer who requires a fundamental pattern to complement the main subject.

Stripes, squares, and dots can usually be integrated into an initial simple background with ease. The necessity for harmony and balance cannot be overly stressed: theme, scale, shape, and style must blend. The central figure must always be considered when the total composition is being planned.

This book offers a large selection of designs that are well suited for embroiderers at all levels of expertise. It can be used as a resource or as a stepping-stone to further your own creativity. Developing designs is exciting and challenging. Put pencil to graph paper, and one filled square leads to another; before you know it, a design emerges. This design becomes a background simply through repetition. Background selection can be achieved through experimentation. Place the chosen graphed designs behind the canvas that contains the central motif. Hold the designs in front of a light so that each will show through and the total effect can be seen. An alternate method is to place your central design against various patterns in this book. You can also work up a few patterns to see which best suits the motif. The process of elimination will help you to determine which is the right background for you to use.

A central figure with many small emanating lines does not take a background easily. Simple wide patterns can possibly be used. A subject contained in a solid form or in compact areas of shape or color is preferable, as it stands out against a background design (see figure C-4), creating a feel of solidarity and of composition flow. There should be sufficient amounts of background to provide continuity and balance. Your desired effect will determine whether you should use contrasting or subtle colors in the background. Any color scheme should harmonize with the foreground figure.

PATTERN GRAPHS

1. Each background design on the following pages can be repeated horizontally, vertically, or at an angle. Color reversal or change of size or proportion are further possible modifications.

2. Each background design consists of a pattern on a field, both of which, represented by circles and squares, are interchangeable.

3. Each box on the graph paper represents one intersection of threads on the canvas. Squint when you view the graphs in order to get the full impact of the designs.

4. Each background design that is employed in a finished project is noted on page 80. Variations of designs are also indicated.

S-14. Mushroom picture. See figure G-222 for pattern. (Stitched by Ronnie Malasky.)

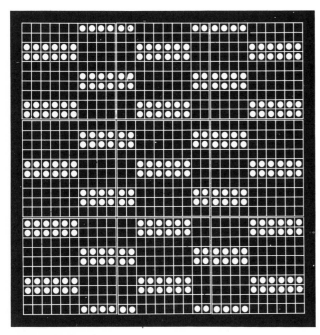

G-1. Basketweave A-1.

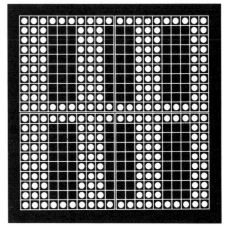

G-3. Bars A-1.

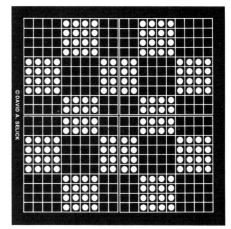

G-4. Basketweave A-2.

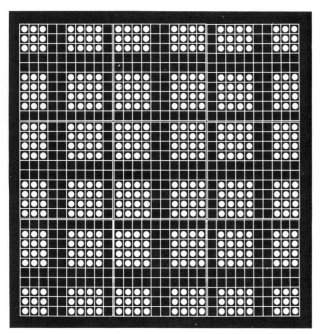

G-2. Windowpanes A-1.

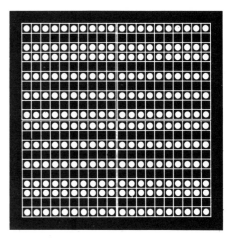

G-5. Stripes A-1.

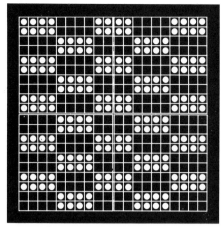

G-6. Basketweave A-3.

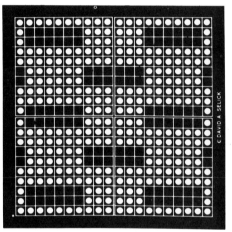

G-7. Bars A-2.

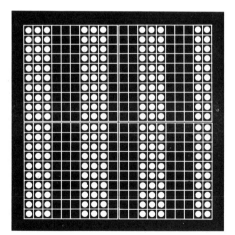

G-8. Stripes A-2.

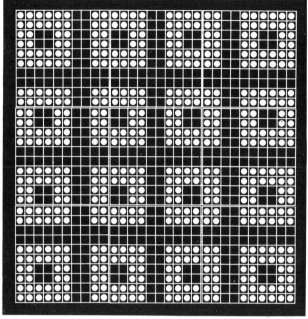

G-9. Boxes A-1.

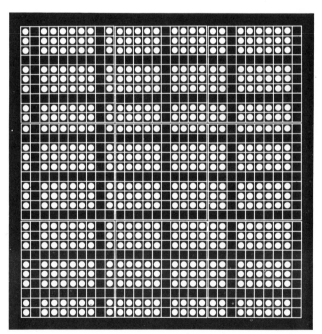

G-10. Windowpanes A-2.

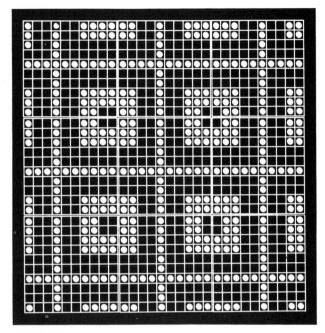

G-11. Boxes A-2.

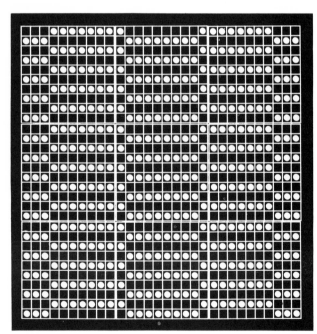

G-12. Cords A-1.

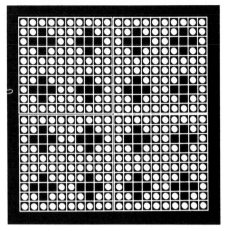

G-13. Crosses A-1.

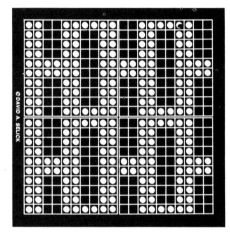

© DAVID A. SELICK

G-14. Bars A-3.

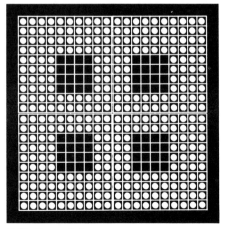

G-15. Boxes A-3.

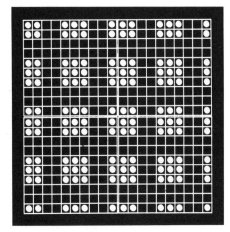

G-16. Boxes A-4.

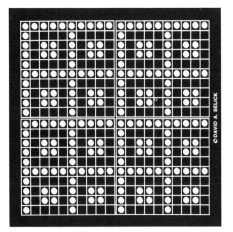

G-17. Boxes A-5.

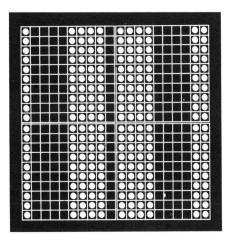

G-18. Stripes A-3.

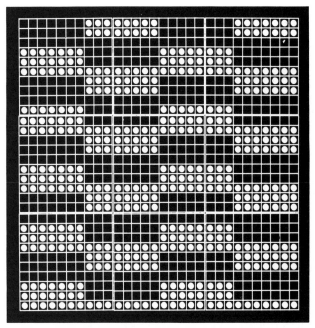

G-19. Basketweave A-4.

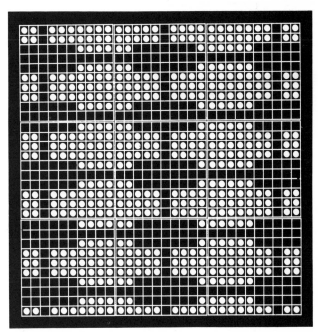

G-20. Lattice A-1.

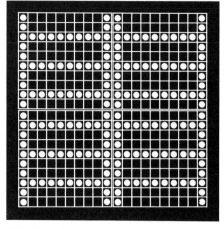

G-23. Bars A-4.

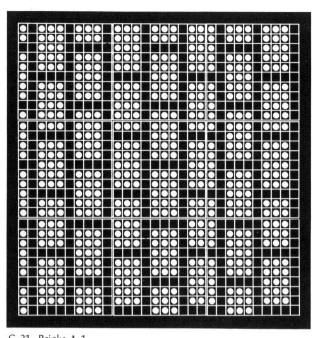

G-21. Bricks A-1.

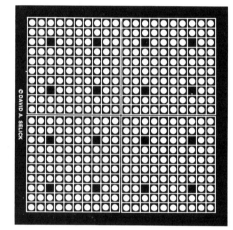

G-24. Dots A-1.

G-22. Basketweave A-5.

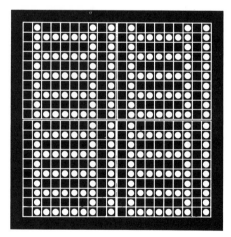

G-25. Ladders A-1.

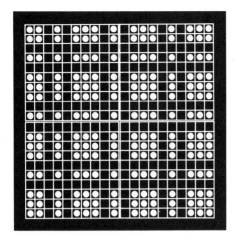

G-26. Plaid A-1.

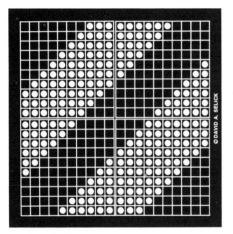

G-27. Diagonals A-1.

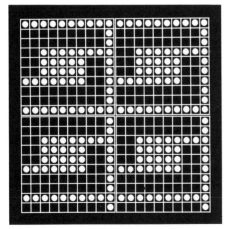

G-28. L's A-1.

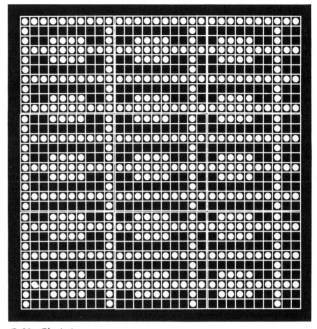

G-29. C's A-1.

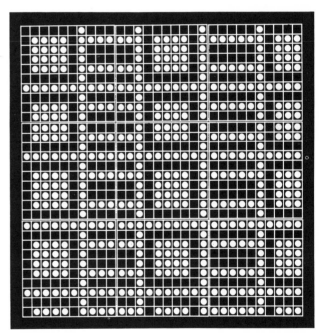

G-30. Boxes A-6.

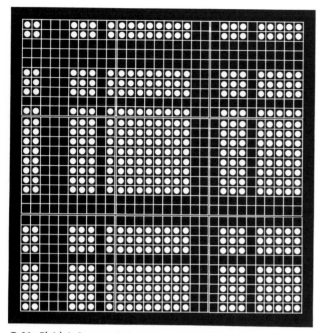

G-31. Plaid A-2.

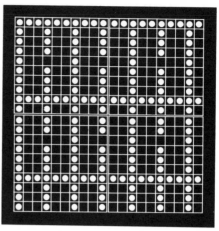

G-33. H's A-1.

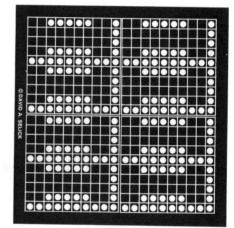

G-34. I's A-1.

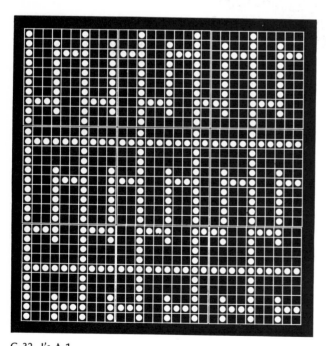

G-32. J's A-1.

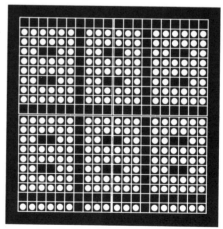

G-35. Dashes A-1.

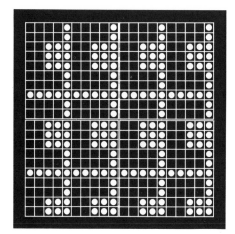

G-36. C's A-2.

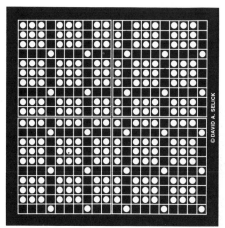

G-37. Basketweave A-6.

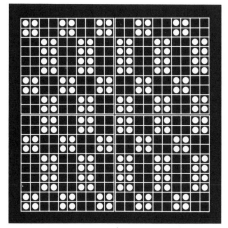

G-38. Basketweave A-7.

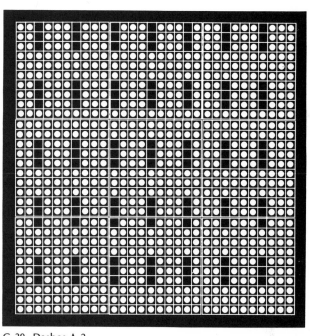

G-39. Dashes A-2.

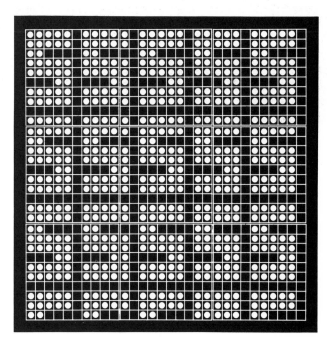

G-40. S's A-1.

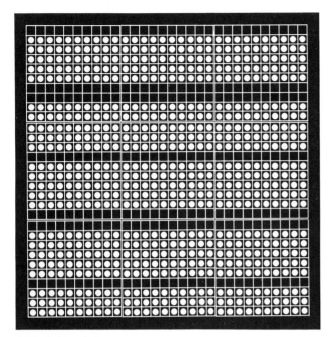

G-41. Stripes A-4.

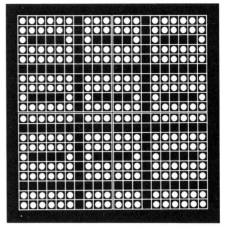

G-43. Dashes A-3.

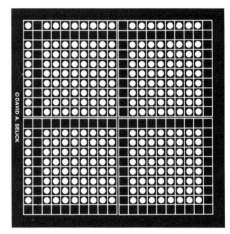

G-44. Windowpanes A-3.

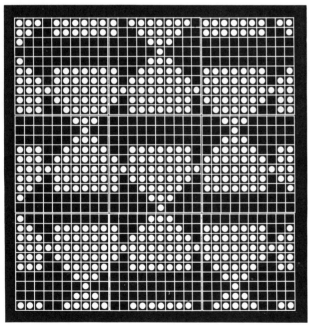

G-42. Arrows A-1.

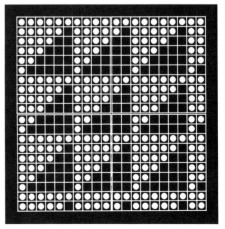

G-45. Triangles A-1.

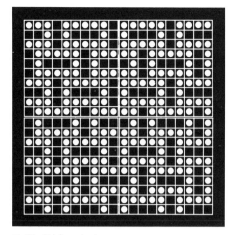

G-46. Dashes A-4.

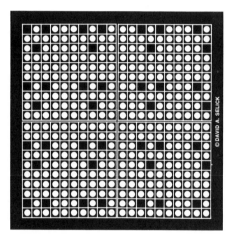

G-47. Dots A-2.

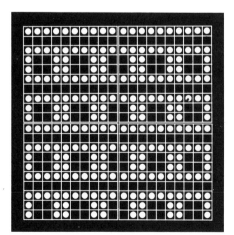

G-48. Stripes A-5.

G-49. Diamonds A-1.

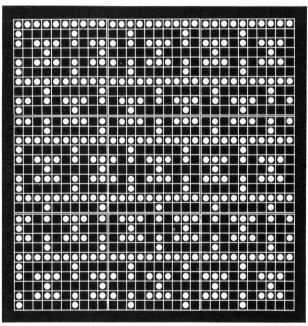

G-50. Links A-1.

©DAVID A. SELICK

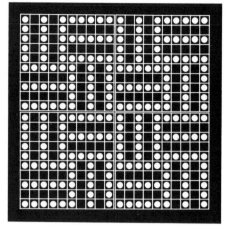
G-53. Ribbons B-1.

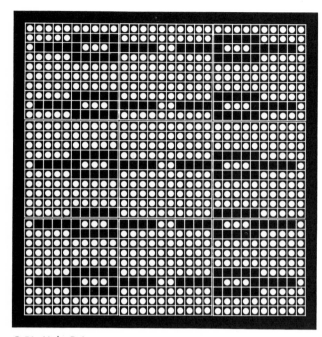
G-51. Links B-1.

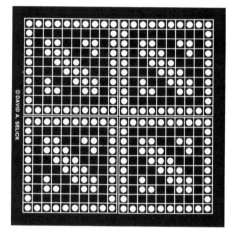
G-54. Boxes B-1.

G-52. Medallions B-1.

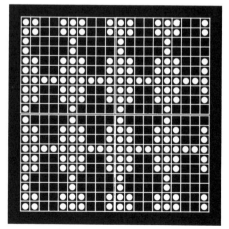
G-55. Crosses B-1.

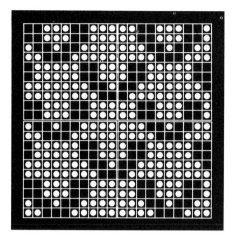

G-56. Horseshoes B-1.

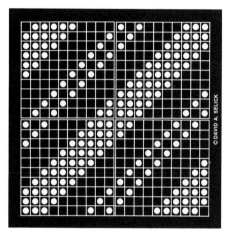

©DAVID A. SELICK

G-57. Diagonals B-1.

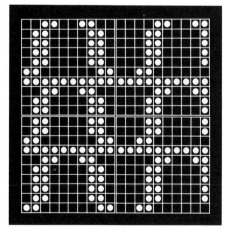

G-58. Bells B-1.

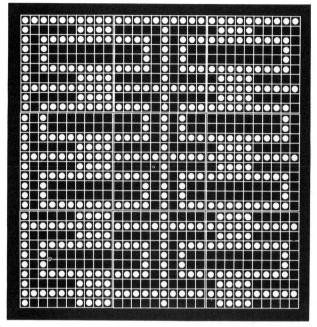

G-59. Bars B-1.

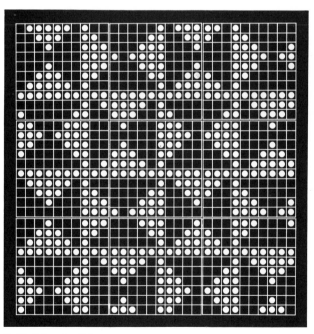

G-60. Triangles B-1.

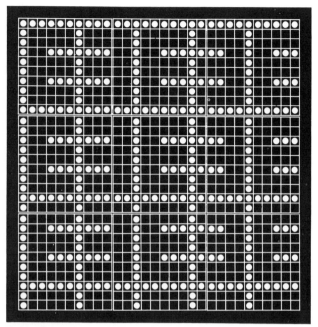

G-61. E's B-1.

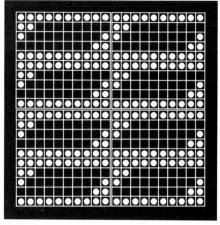

G-63. Bars B-2.

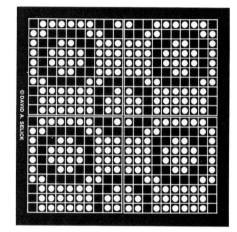

G-64. Circles B-1.

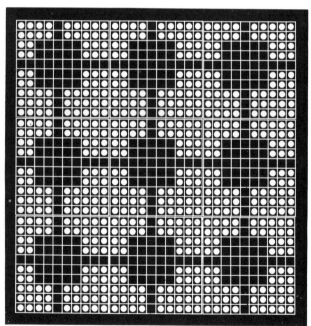

G-62. Lattice B-1.

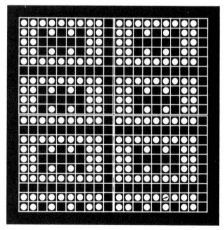

G-65. Indian B-1.

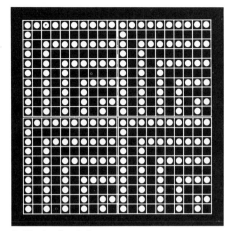

G-66. Angles B-1.

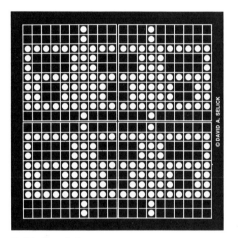

G-67. Bars B-3.

©DAVID A. SELICK

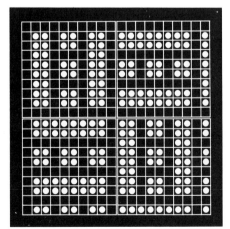

G-68. Ribbons B-2.

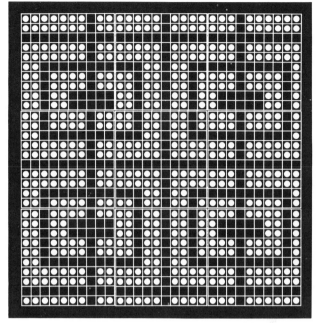

G-69. C's B-1.

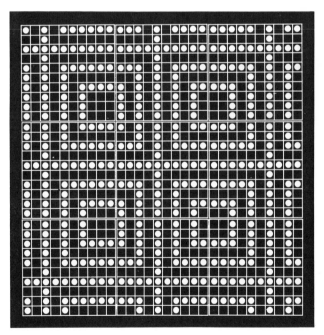

G-70. Boxes B-2.

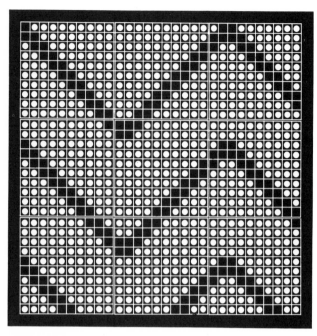

G-71. Zigzags B-1.

G-72. Ribbons B-3.

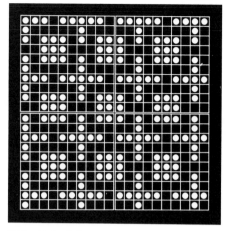

G-73. Links B-2.

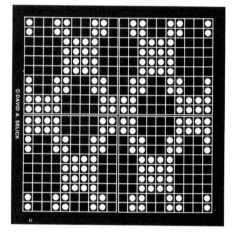

G-74. Diamonds B-1.

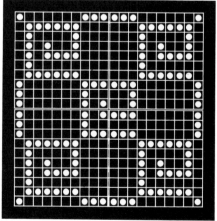

G-75. Boxes B-3.

24

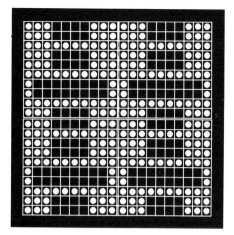

G-76. Bars B-4.

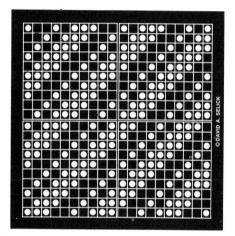

G-77. Diagonals B-2.

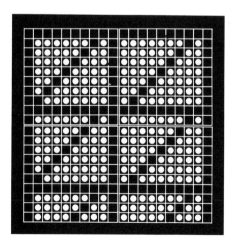

G-78. Triangles B-2.

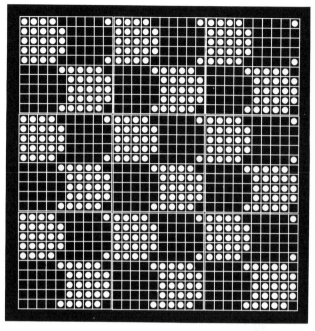

G-79. Basketweave B-1.

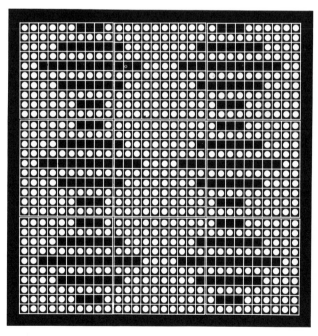

G-80. Bars B-5.

G-81. Pinwheels B-1.

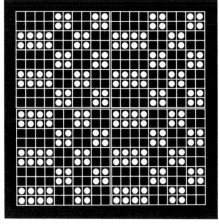

G-83. Basketweave B-2.

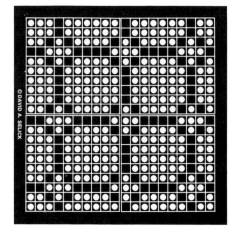

G-84. Lattice B-2.

G-82. Ribbons B-4.

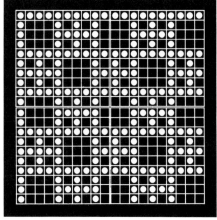

G-85. Boxes B-4.

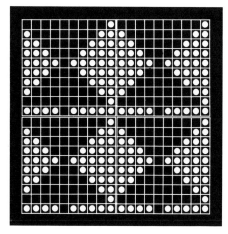

G-86. Diamonds B-2.

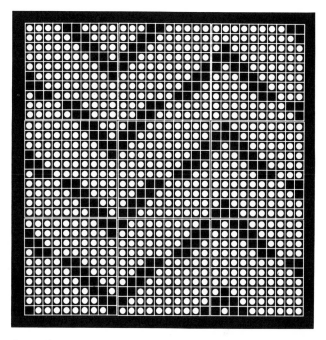

G-89. Chevrons B-1.

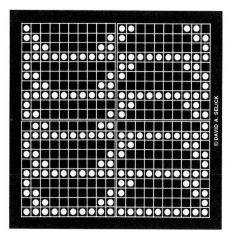

G-87. Bars B-6.

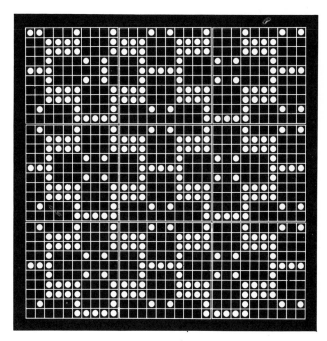

G-90. Crosses B-2.

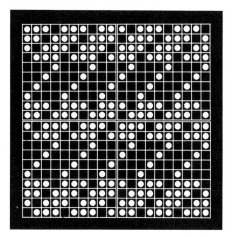

G-88. Houndstooth B-1.

© DAVID A. SELICK

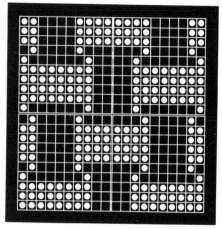

G-91. Lattice B-3.

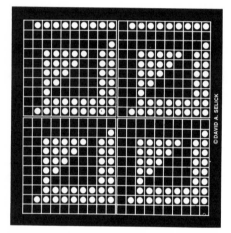

G-92. Diamonds B-3.

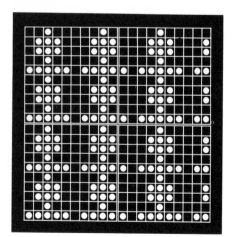

G-93. I's B-1.

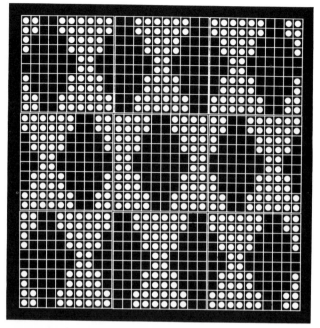

G-94. Triangles B-3.

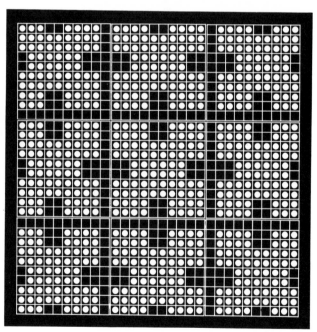

G-95. I's B-2.

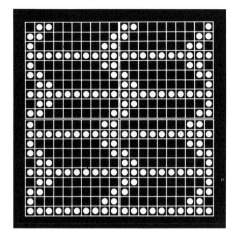

G-96. Bars B-7.

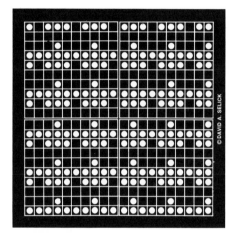

G-97. Stripes B-1.

©DAVID A. SELICK

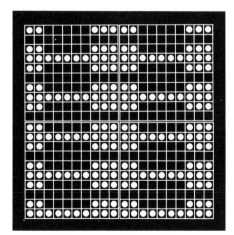

G-98. Lattice B-4.

G-99. Lattice B-5.

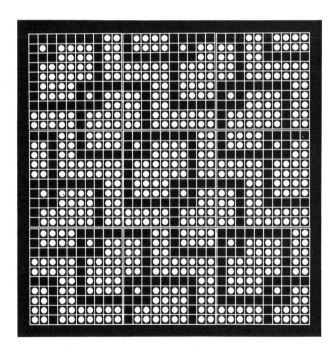

G-100. Links B-3.

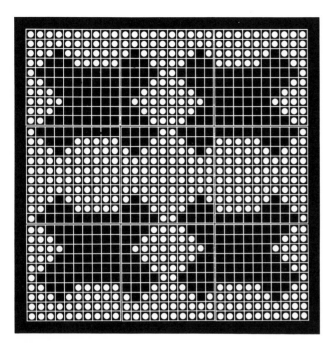

G-101. X's B-1.

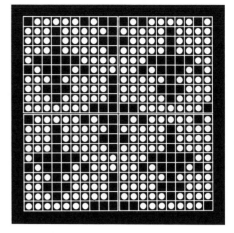

G-103. Fleur-de-lis B-1.

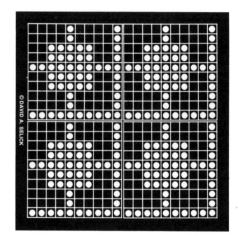

© DAVID A. SELICK

G-104. L's B-1.

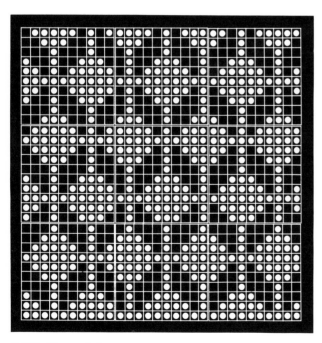

G-102. Zigzags B-2.

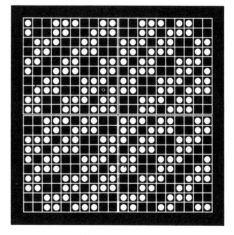

G-105. Diagonals B-3.

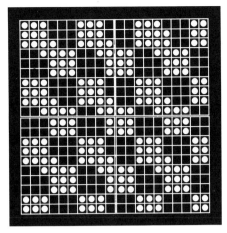

G-106. Twill B-1.

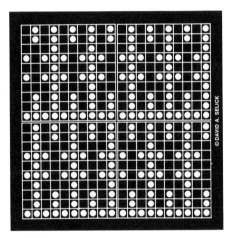

©DAVID A. SELICK

G-107. Indian B-2.

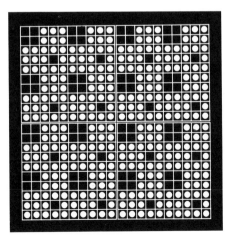

G-108. Boxes B-5.

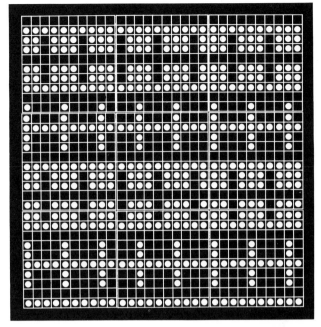

G-109. Tracks B-1.

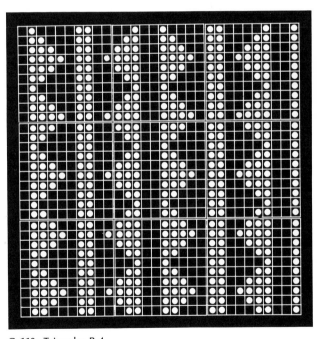

G-110. Triangles B-4.

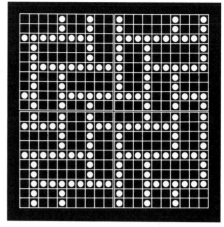

G-113. Zigzags B-3.

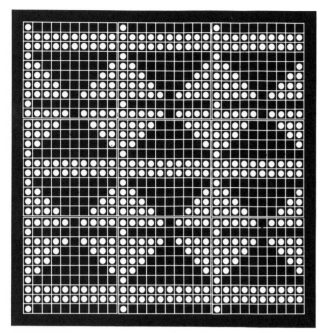

G-111. Indian B-3.

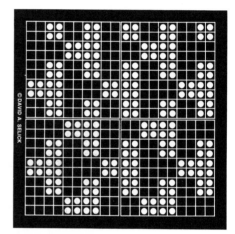

G-114. Twill B-2.

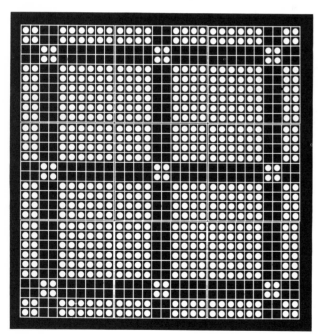

G-112. Boxes B-6.

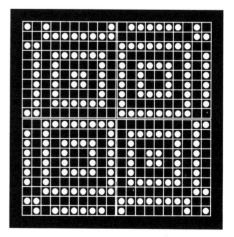

G-115. Boxes B-7.

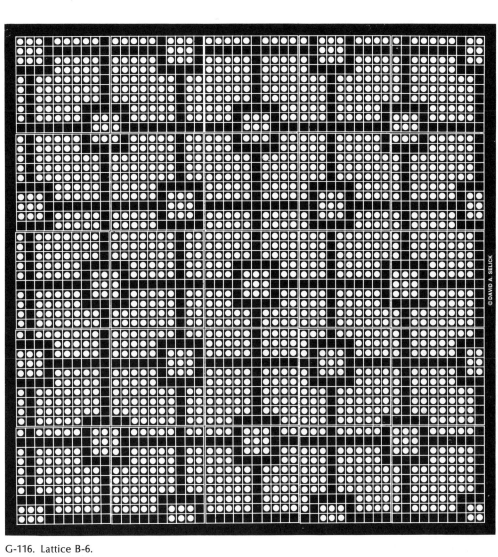

G-116. Lattice B-6.

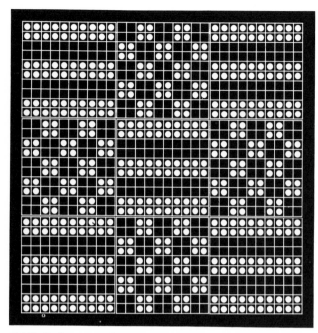

G-117. Basketweave C-1.

G-118. Zigzags C-1.

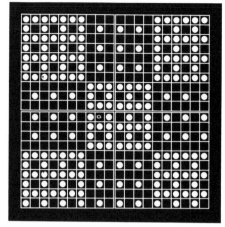

G-119. Boxes C-1.

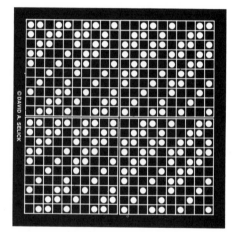

G-120. Diagonals C-1.

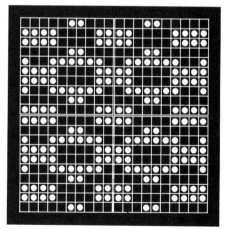

G-121. Links C-1.

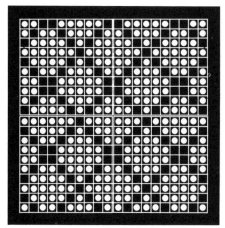

G-122. Diamonds C-1.

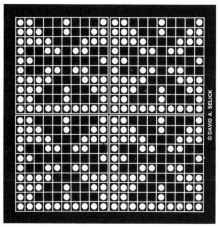

G-123. Indian C-1.

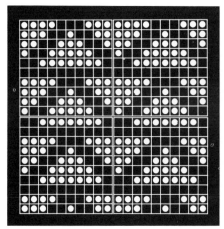

G-124. Triangles C-1.

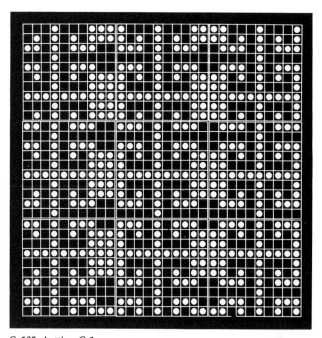

G-125. Lattice C-1.

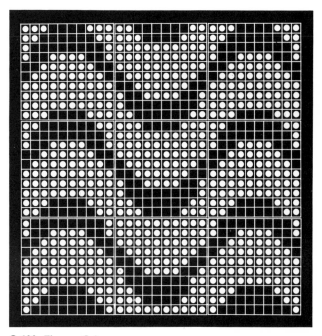

G-126. Zigzags C-2.

©DAVID A. SELICK

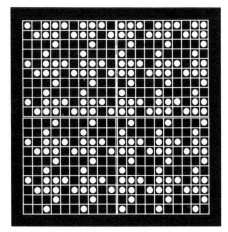

G-127. Cane C-1.

G-131. Plaid C-1.

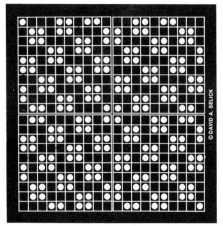

G-128. Medallions C-1.

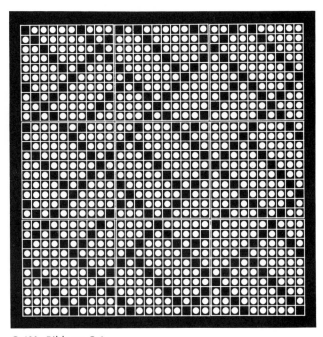

G-130. Ribbons C-1.

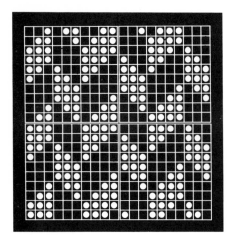

G-129. Twill C-1.

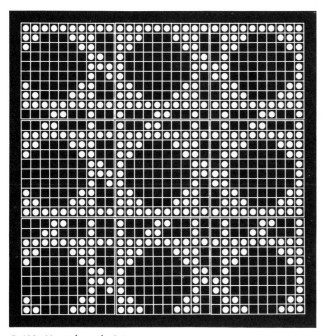

G-132. Houndstooth C-1.

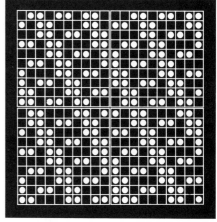

G-134. Herringbone C-1.

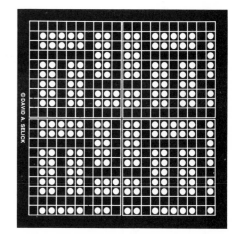

G-135. Flowers C-1.

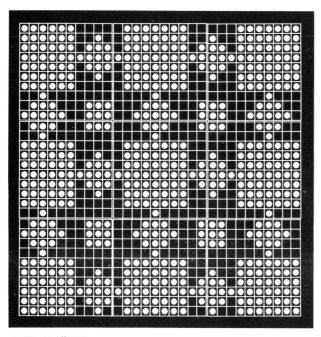

G-133. Twill C-2.

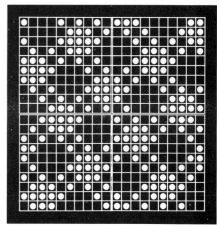

G-136. Lattice C-2.

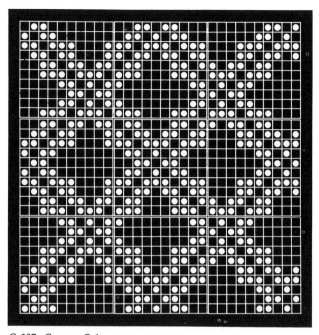

G-137. Crosses C-1.

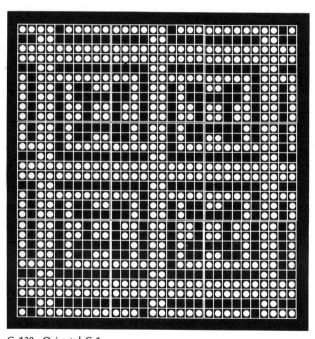

G-138. Oriental C-1.

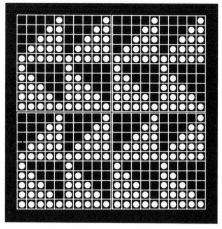

G-139. Triangles C-2.

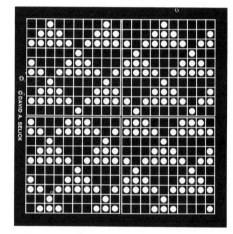

G-140. Triangles C-3.

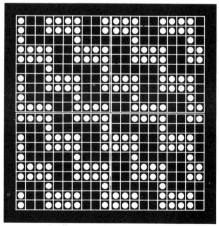

G-141. Twill C-3.

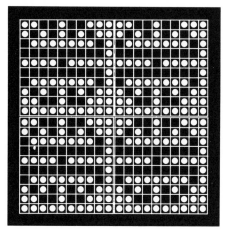

G-142. Oriental C-2.

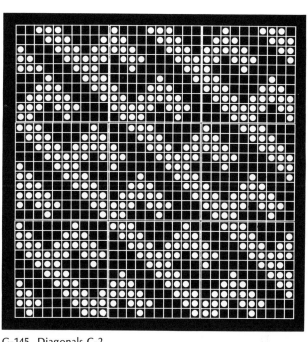

G-145. Diagonals C-2.

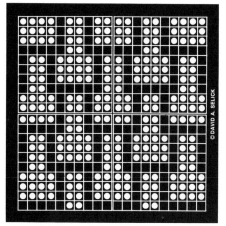

G-143. T's C-1.

©DAVID A. SELICK

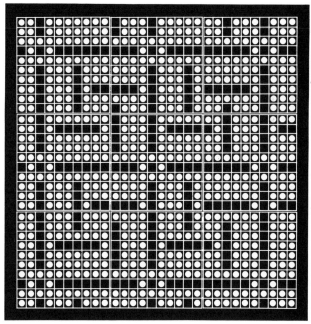

G-146. Lattice C-3.

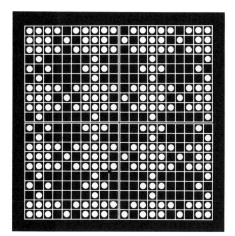

G-144. Plaid C-2.

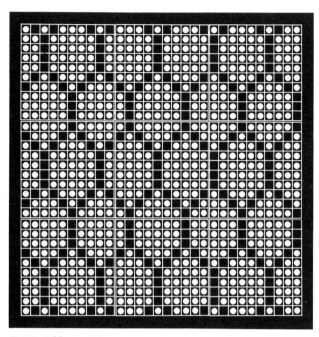

G-150. Ribbons C-2.

G-151. Stripes C-1.

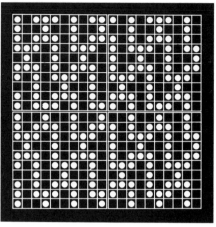

G-147. Honeycombs C-1.

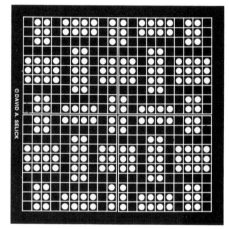

G-148. Herringbone C-2.

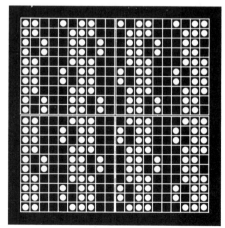

G-149. Z's C-1.

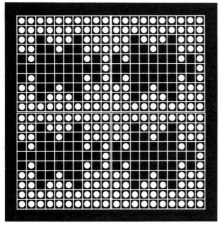

G-152. Indian C-2.

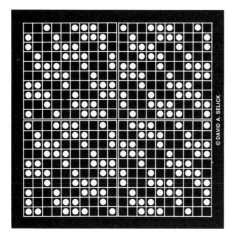

G-153. Twill C-4.

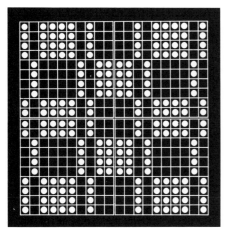

G-154. Basketweave C-2.

G-155. Herringbone C-3.

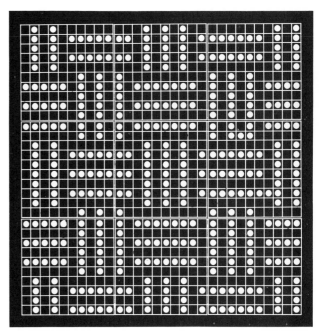

G-156. Ribbons C-3.

© DAVID A. SELICK

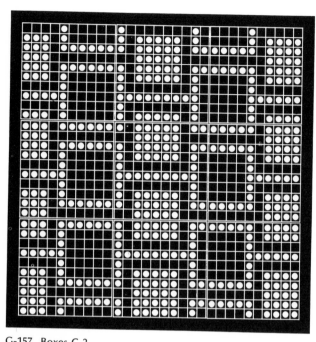

G-157. Boxes C-2.

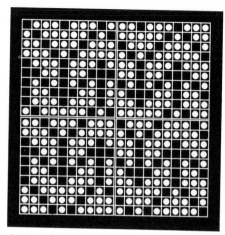

G-159. Chevrons C-1.

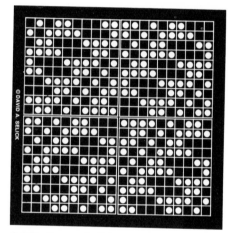

G-160. Diagonals C-3.

G-158. Herringbone C-4.

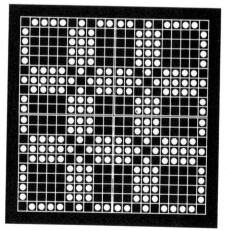

G-161. Boxes C-3.

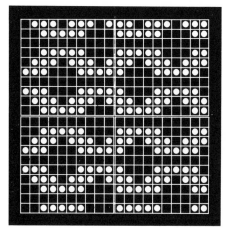

G-162. Diamonds C-2.

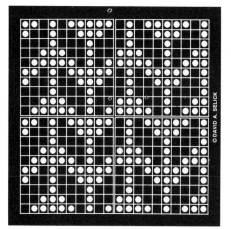

G-163. Herringbone C-5.

©DAVID A. SELICK

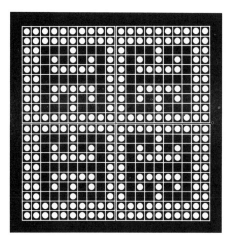

G-164. Oriental C-3.

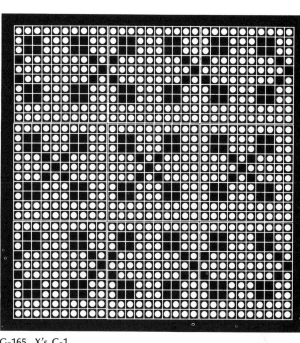

G-165. X's C-1.

G-166. Boxes C-4.

G-167. Zigzags C-3.

G-168. Arrows C-1.

© DAVID A. SELICK

G-169. Diagonals D-1.

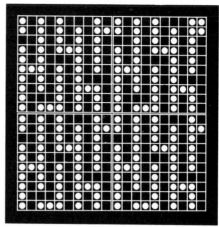

G-171. Lattice D-1.

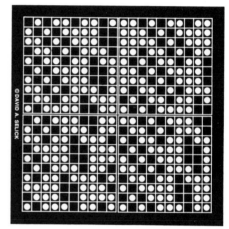

G-172. Diagonals D-2.

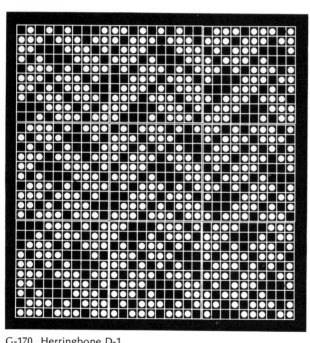

G-170. Herringbone D-1.

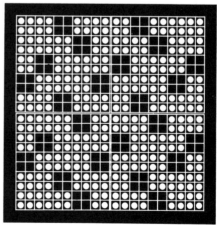

G-173. Boxes D-1.

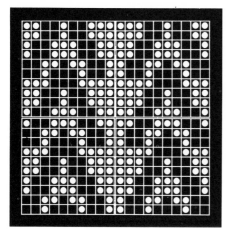

G-174. Lattice D-2.

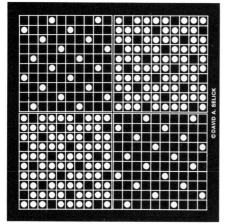

©DAVID A. SELICK

G-175. Diagonals D-3.

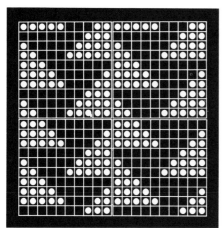

G-176. Triangles D-1.

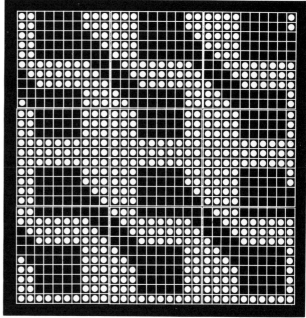

G-177. Boxes D-2.

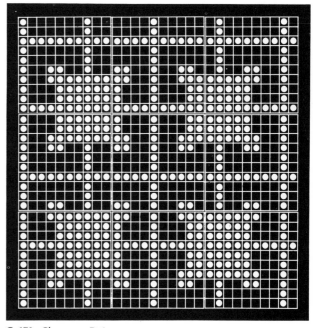

G-178. Chevrons D-1.

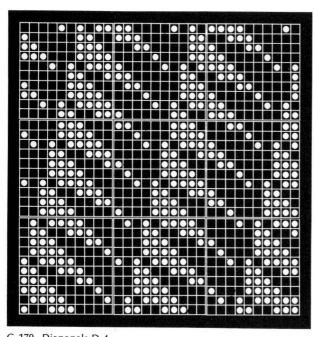

G-179. Diagonals D-4.

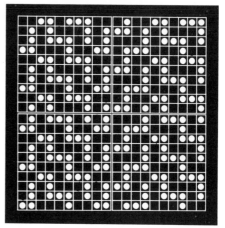

G-181. Zigzags D-1.

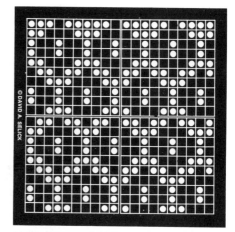

G-182. Diamonds D-1.

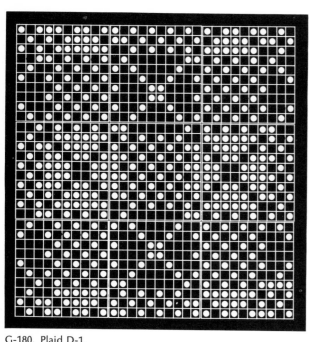

G-180. Plaid D-1.

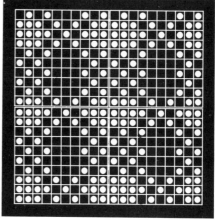

G-183. Plaid D-2.

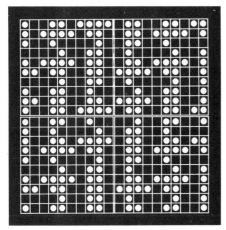

G-184. Houndstooth D-1.

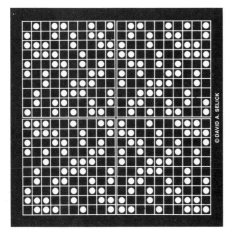

G-185. Diagonals D-5.

©DAVID A. SELICK

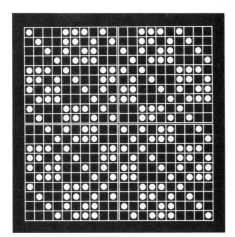

G-186. Triangles D-2.

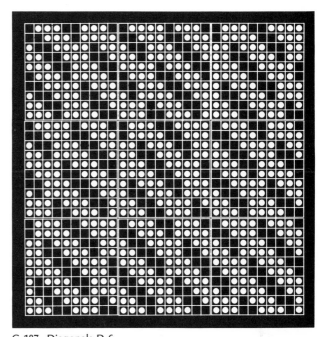

G-187. Diagonals D-6.

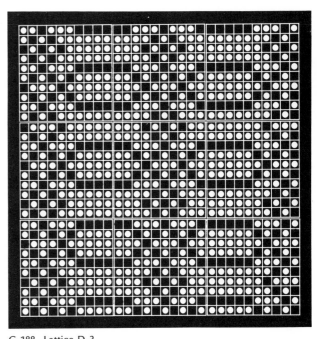

G-188. Lattice D-3.

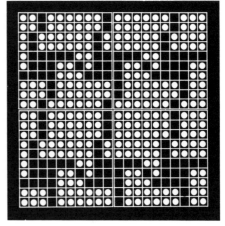

G-191. Houndstooth D-2.

G-189. Scallops D-1.

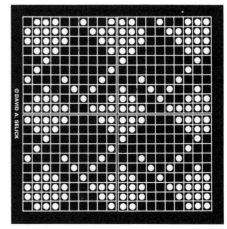

G-192. Diamonds D-2.

G-190. Diagonals D-7.

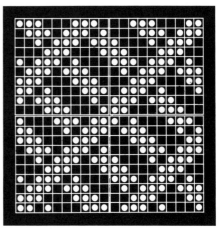

G-193. Diagonals D-8.

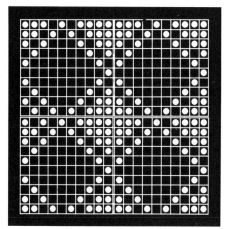

G-194. Diamonds D-3.

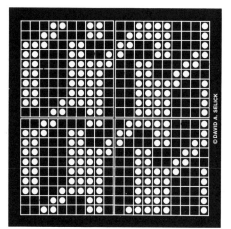

G-195. S's D-1.

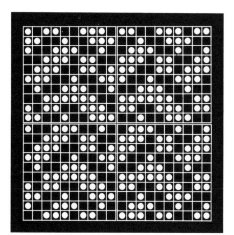

G-196. Basketweave D-1.

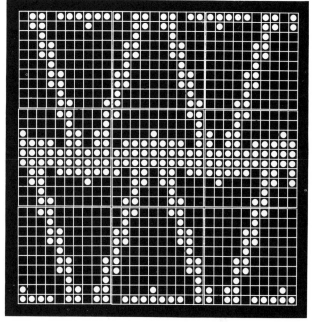

G-197. Arrows D-1.

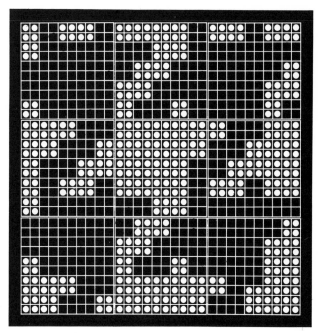

G-198. Houndstooth D-3.

© DAVID A. SELICK

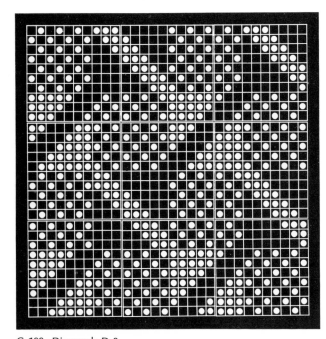

G-199. Diagonals D-9.

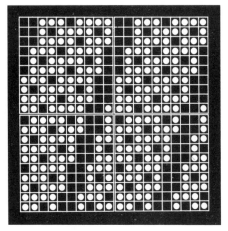

G-201. Diagonals D-10.

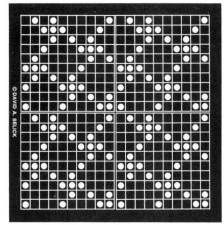

G-202. Diamonds D-4.

G-200. Pinwheels D-1.

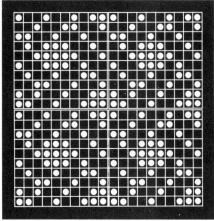

G-203. Ribbons D-1.

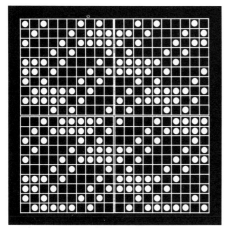

G-204. Diagonals D-11.

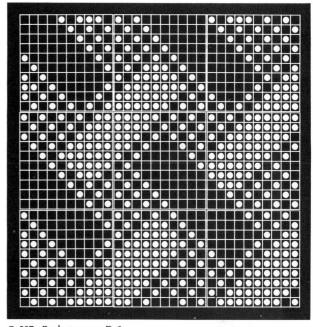

G-207. Basketweave D-2.

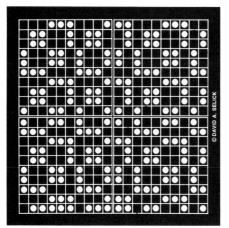

G-205. Boxes D-3.

G-208. Diagonals D-12.

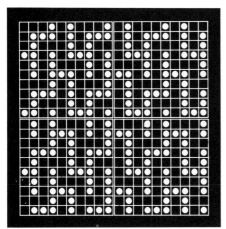

G-206. Lattice D-4.

©DAVID A. SELICK

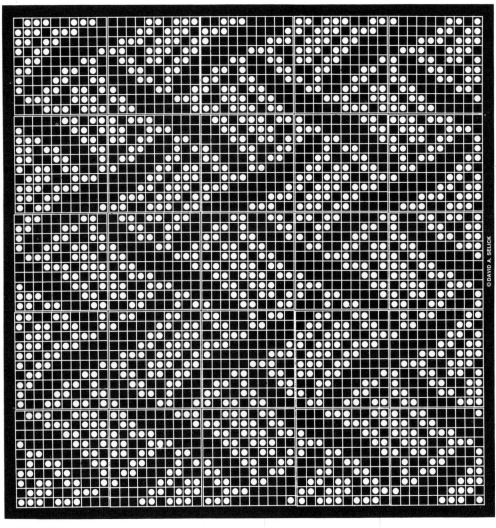

G-209. Ribbons D-2.

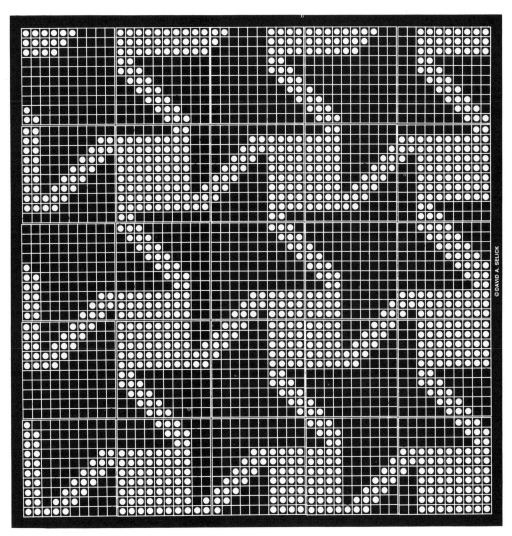

G-210. Pinwheels D-2.

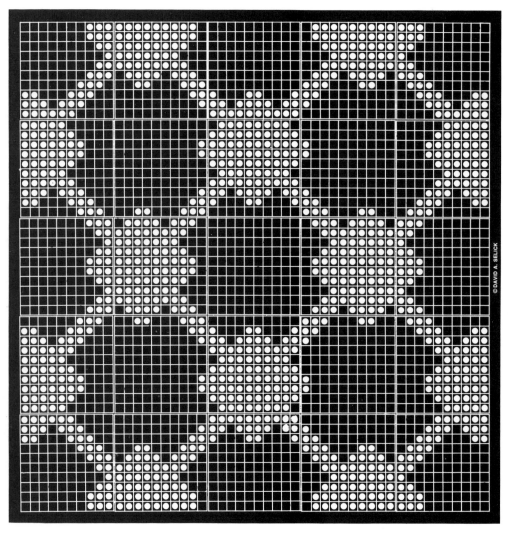

G-211. Lattice D-5.

G-212. Herringbone D-2.

G-213. S's D-2.

G-214. Oriental D-1.

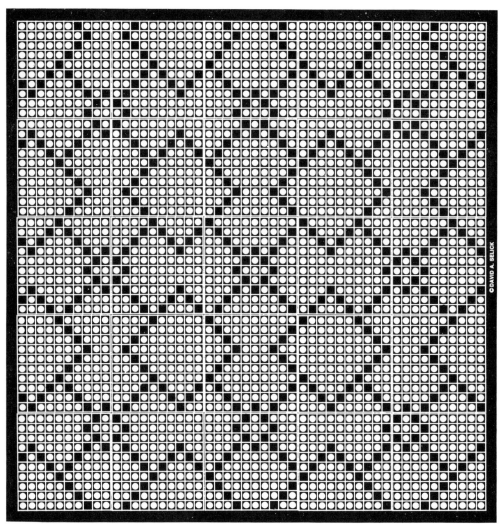

G-215. Diamonds D-5.

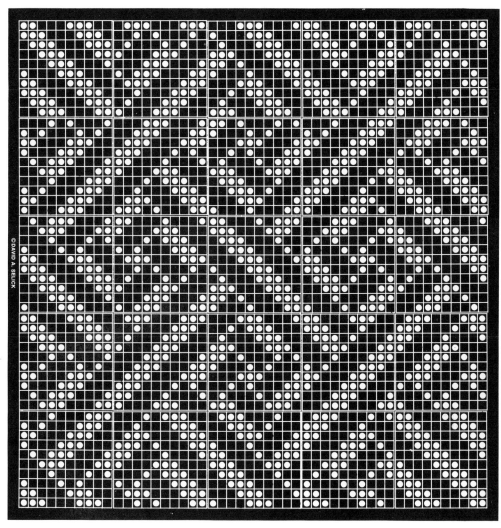

G-216. Ribbons D-3.

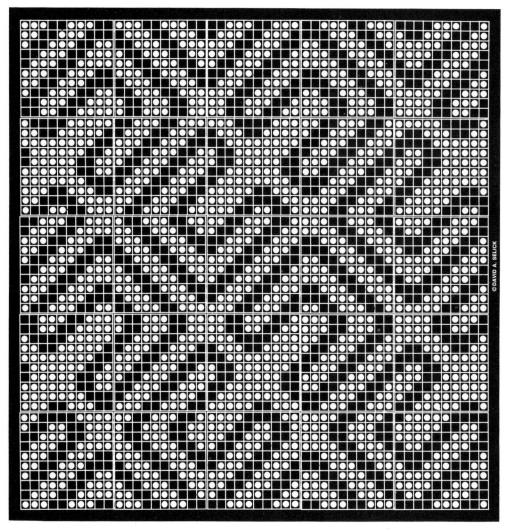

G-217. U's D-1.

©DAVID A. SELICK

G-218. C's D-1.

G-219. Ribbons D-4.

G-220. Ribbons D-5.

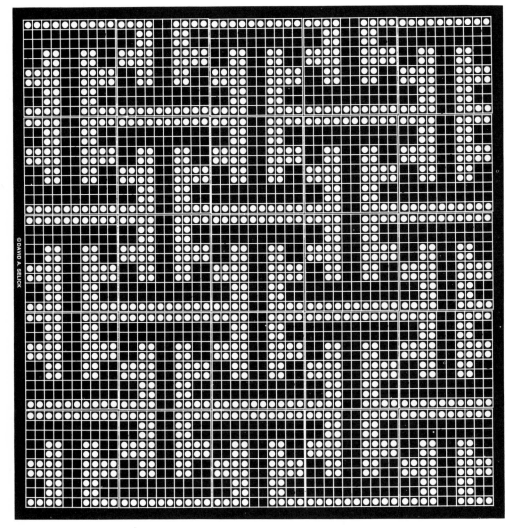

G-221. Oriental D-2.

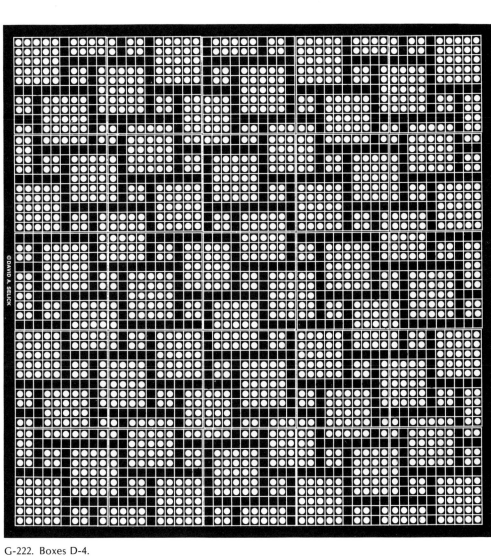

G-222. Boxes D-4.

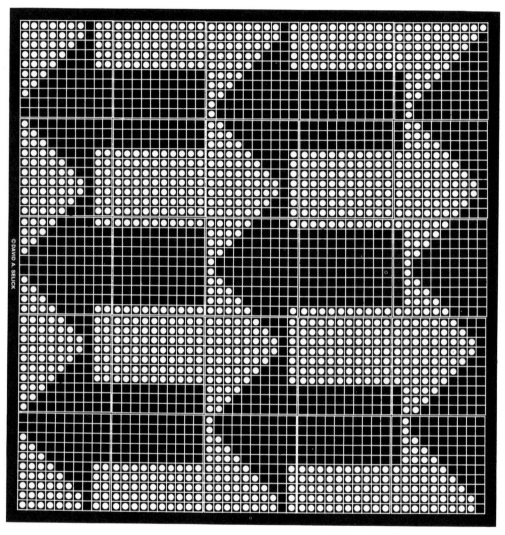

G-223. Arrows D-2.

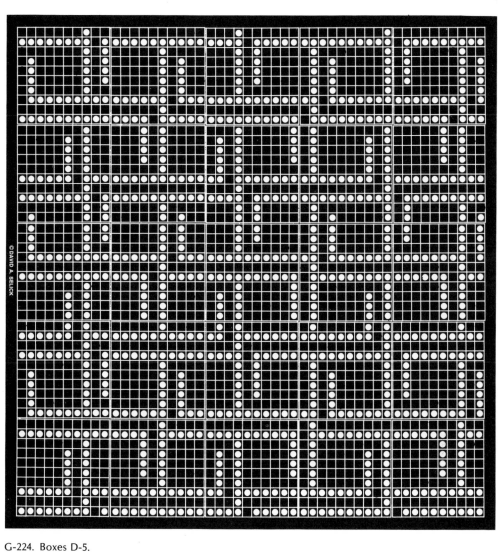

G-224. Boxes D-5.

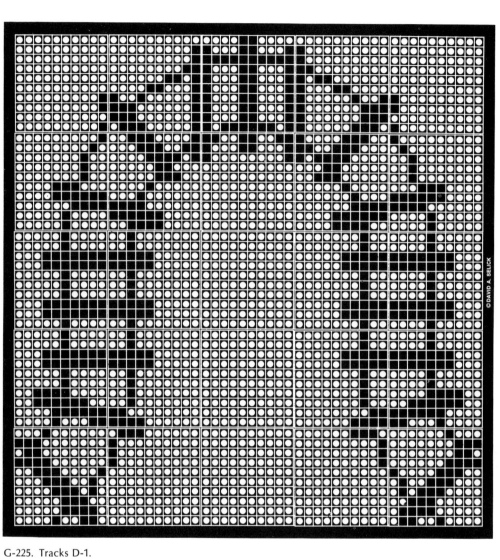

G-225. Tracks D-1.

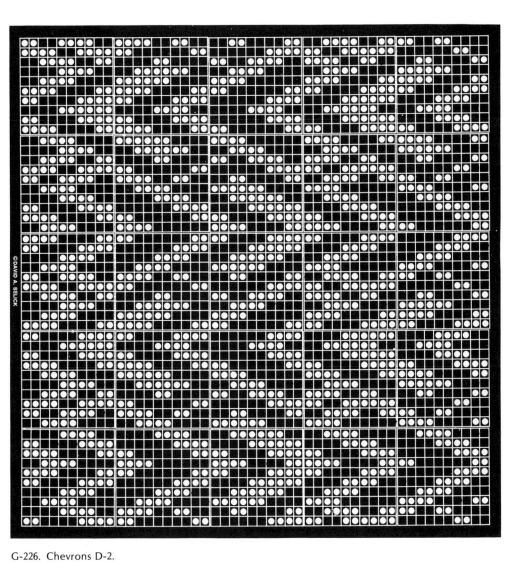

G-226. Chevrons D-2.

G-227. Z's D-1.

G-228. Diamonds D-6.

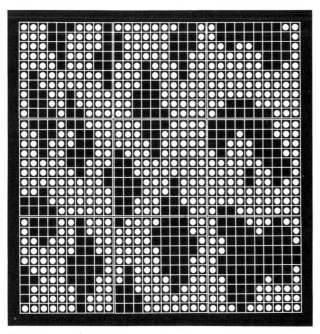

G-229. Leopard D-1.

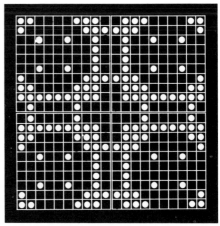

G-231. Medallions D-1.

G-232. Windowpane D-1.

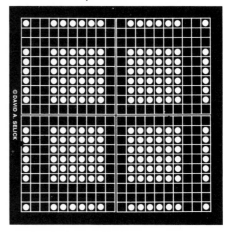

G-230. Stripes D-1.

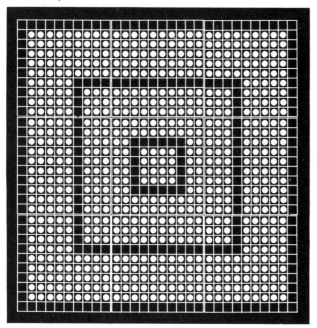

G-233. Tweed D-1.

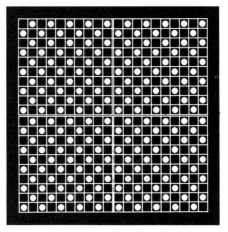

Figure G-229 is a portion of the random repeat used in figure C-9. Its individual patterns, asymmetrically placed on the field, give you freedom of expression to stitch. Fill the entire canvas background by varying the spots in size, shape, and position, using this sole theme to reproduce the natural effect of leopard skin.

Figure G-230 is a simple stripe that has been mitered with its central design. The stripe produces a box effect.

Figure G-232 is on a canvas that was cut and held while it was worked at a 45° angle, giving the diagonal cross-lines and the squares smooth edges. If the canvas had been held in the conventional manner, the diagonal cross-lines and the squares would have appeared jagged.

Figure G-233 produces a tweed effect. This is accomplished by working alternately colored diagonal rows in a backstitch.

STITCHED PATTERNS

The following section contains stitched samples of some of the graph designs. Three designs from each level of complexity are shown.

S-15. I shoulderbag and change purse. (Stitched by Irene Marton.)

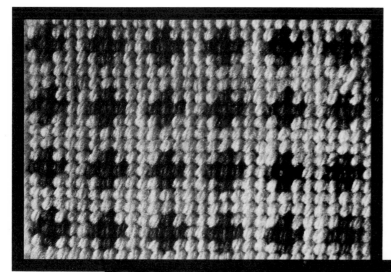

S-1. Crosses A-1.

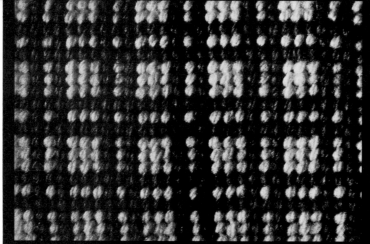

S-2. Plaid A-1.

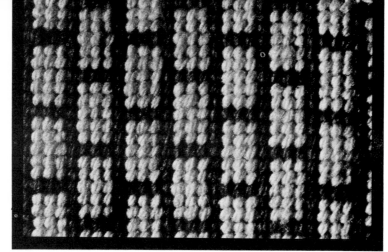

S-3. Bricks A-1.

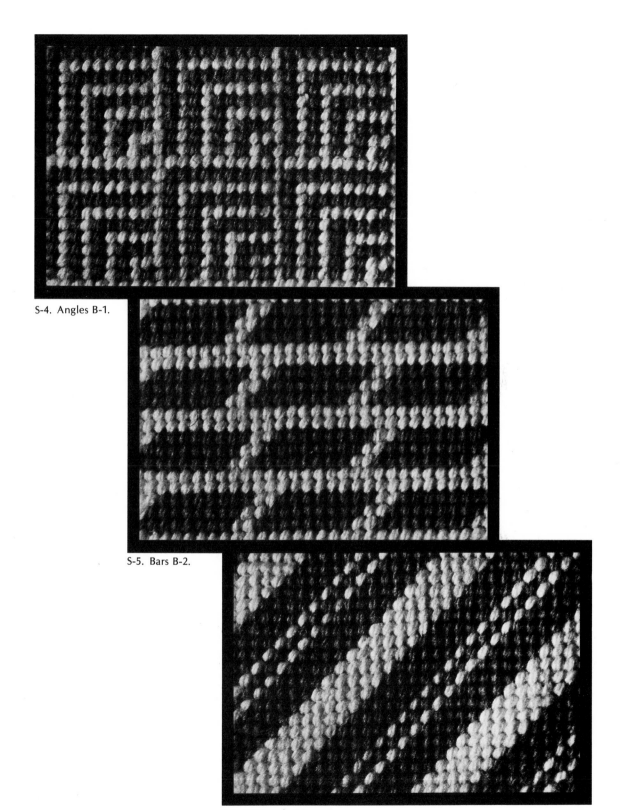

S-4. Angles B-1.

S-5. Bars B-2.

S-6. Diagonals B-1.

S-7. Basketweave C-2.

S-8. Twill C-2.

S-9. Herringbone C-3.

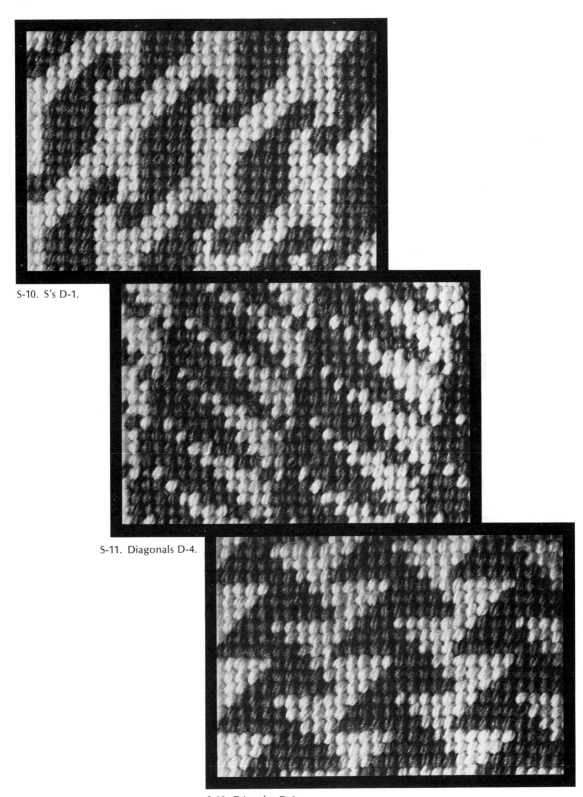

S-10. S's D-1.

S-11. Diagonals D-4.

S-12. Triangles D-1.

PROJECT PORTFOLIO

S-13. Mushroom picture. (Stitched by Ronnie Malasky.)

The following section contains color photographs of finished projects. Below is a key to the project, the graph design and technique used, and the stitched sample, if any, of the pattern:

Project	Graph	Technique	Stitched Sample
C-1	G-198	basketweave	
C-2	G-179	basketweave	S-11
C-3	G-45	continental	
C-4	G-190	background: basketweave	
		central design: cashmere	
C-5	G-117	basketweave	
C-6	G-82	basketweave	
C-7	G-140	basketweave	
C-8	G-230	basketweave	
C-9	G-229	basketweave	
C-10	G-209	basketweave	
C-11	G-79	basketweave	
C-12			
(left)	G-232	white background: scotch,	
		blue background: basketweave,	
		dark fur and features: crewelpoint,	
		remainder: basketweave	
(left center)	G-95	basketweave	
(right center)	G-155	basketweave	S-9
(right)	G-213	basketweave	
C-13	G-176	basketweave	S-12
C-14			
(left)	G-233	backstitch	
(right)	G-145	basketweave	
C-15	G-91	basketweave	
C-16	G-44	basketweave	
		floral centers: petit point	
C-17	G-21 (variation)	basketweave	S-3
C-18	G-127	basketweave	
C-19	G-217	basketweave	
C-20			
(left)	G-18	continental	
(right)	G-26	continental	S-2
C-21	G-41	continental	
C-22			
(left)	G-42	continental	
(right)	G-225	white background: brick	
		remainder: basketweave	
C-23	G-221	basketweave	
C-24	G-148	tweed effect in background backstitch,	
		remainder: basketweave	
		central design: basketweave	

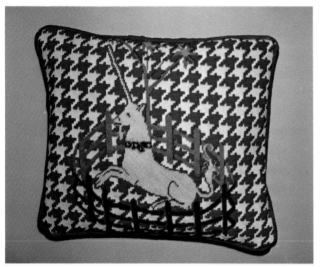

C-1. Unicorn pillow.

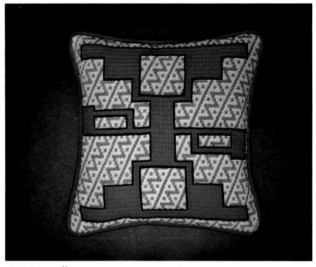

C-4. Inca pillow.

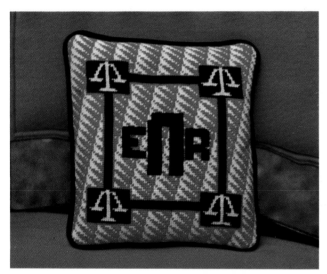

C-2. Scale of Justice pillow. (Courtesy of the Ellen and Richard Nassberg collection. Photo by Richard T. Nassberg.)

C-5. Eagle pillow. (Courtesy of the Ellen and Richard Nassberg collection. Photo by Richard T. Nassberg.)

C-3. City Retreat. (Designed and stitched in quickpoint by Frederic Marton at 8 years of age.)

C-6. Pagoda pillow. (Stitched by Barbara Weber.)

C-7. Eyeglass case. (Stitched by Gerri Kurzman.)

C-10. Seashells pillow.

C-8. Mitered tulip pillow.

C-11. Seahorse box. (Courtesy of the Harriet and Robert Cohen collection.)

C-9. Tiger pillow.

C-12. From left to right: monkey pillow (stitched by Barbara Weber), I shoulderbag (stitched by Irene Marton), herringbone-poppy pillow, triangle pillow.

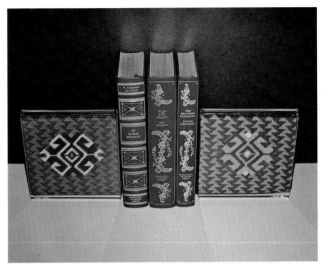

C-13. Indian bookends.

C-16. Windowpane-daffodil pillow.

C-14. From left to right: tweed pillow, Chinese-symbol cushion.

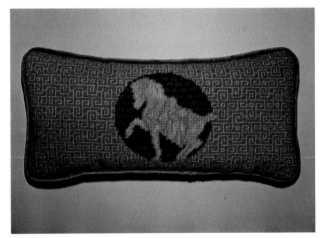

C-17. Equestrian pillow.

C-15. Lattice-daffodil pillow.

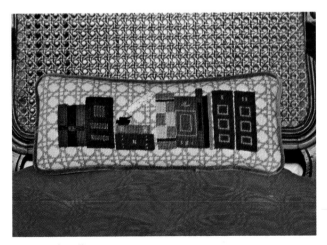

C-18. Books pillow.

C-19. Lyre pillow.

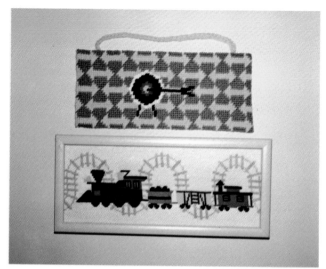

C-22. From top to bottom: target wallhanging (stitched by Matthew Selick at 8 years of age, with a little help from Steven Selick at 6 years of age), train picture.

C-20. From left to right: scissors case (stitched by Willa Trestman), friends pillow (stitched by Willa Trestman).

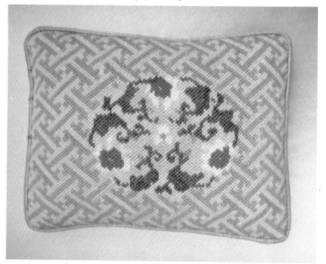

C-23. Henriette's medallion.

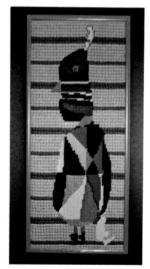

C-21. Monster picture. (Designed and stitched in quick-point by Frederic Marton at 7½ years of age.)

C-24. Dinosaur pillow.

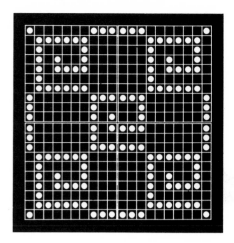

HOW TO CHOOSE KITS AND OTHER MATERIALS

Needlepointers may have several reasons for not designing a total canvas. Some may find commercial products to suit their needs. Others may be hesitant to attempt an entire project. Still others may be pressed for time or inspiration. A kit or a painted canvas can be the answer, and incorporating a background design on a commercial canvas provides an easy means of individualizing the work. Canvas with an overall factory-printed repeating pattern is available by the yard, and your own central design can be superimposed as another creative alternative. The background, however, will not be original: it is certain to be duplicated, although not necessarily in your chosen colors.

KITS

You can individualize your kit, differentiate it from your neighbor's by incorporating a background, symbol, or design that reflects your interests or those of the person to whom you may be presenting it. Using your own background instantly sets your canvas apart from all other kits with the same central design. It is your most basic, obvious, and profound variation.

Keep in mind that kits differ greatly in quality. Cost does not always reflect the value of the contents. Canvas, yarn, and the manner in which the design is applied should be considered. Background designs require a fairly large area of blank peripheral canvas. To select a kit, first make sure that there is enough space to stitch at least two repeats around the central design. If you are using a small repeat, a pleasing amount

of background area should be available to maintain balance. Four rows for seams and an area for blocking are also essential.

A shiny canvas generally contains strands that are hardier and less likely to split. Have it taped. Knots and slubs are undesirable. Ascertain whether the canvas is the gauge that you desire. Always check the mesh count: the number of horizontal and vertical threads per inch (centimeter) should correspond with the canvas number. Grids should be parallel. Interlocking canvas may not unweave as easily as regular canvas, but it can still unravel. It also can catch your yarn more readily, since sharp edges split it, causing it to fray.

Yarn quality and quantity should be considered. The strands should be strong with a glossy finish: avoid knots. Never assume that all strands of one color match: check them in daylight to be sure that all are from the same dye lot. It is vital that the yarn colors and the painted portion of the canvas be waterproof. A clear acrylic spray—a fixative—can be applied to the painted canvas if you are in doubt. Spray lightly: a heavy dose may cause the paint to bleed.

The yarn and the canvas should correspond: openings in the canvas should be filled completely without crowding or distortion. Make sure that the correct thickness of yarn is supplied. Enough yarn should be provided to complete the work with some extra to correct errors and to provide for a seam allowance. Select a second color compatible with the background color provided in order to stitch a patterned-background design. The half-cross-stitch, for example, requires approximately one-third the amount of yarn needed for the continental or basketweave stitch. If the manufacturer suggests that the half-cross be used, there may be too little yarn for the other two tent stitches or for most special stitches. You may have just enough yarn to work the half-cross, which is a weak and awkward stitch.

Small open spaces in the midst of the central design are undesirable for patterned-background designs. They are difficult to fill with the proper coordinating count; they look picky and give the canvas a busy appearance. Colored intersections of the canvas grids should be marked clearly. This is especially important for a geometric design, in which one erroneous stitch would throw the entire pattern.

The background patterns should be compatible with the central design of your kit in color, style, and size. The object and the spacing of the background design should balance and be in accord with the central design. Do not permit the background to overwhelm the central design: it should become an integral part of the entire composition. Coordinate the background colors with those that are stitched or painted on the canvas. You can always substitute new yarn for that included in the kit, but this is expensive: the original can be kept for the future. The colors should also coordinate with those in the room in which the finished work will be placed. Different color schemes will create different effects in the same design.

Special effects can further individualize your kit. Specific stitches (see the monkey pillow in figure C-12, the train picture in figure C-22, and figures S-13 and S-14), superimposed crewelwork or crewelpoint (see the change purse in figure S-15, the friends pillow in figure C-20, and the monkey pillow in figure C-12, and mixtures of yarn to create new blends in color or texture (see figures C-15 and C-16) are possibilities. Mitering is intricate but gives your work an entirely different look (see figure C-8). Silk or metallic threads highlight details and give dimension in an unusual manner (see the collar in figure C-1 and the strings in figure C-19). See "How to Select Patterned Backgrounds" for details.

Mixtures of yarn can create new blends of color and texture. Combining various hues of yarn within each strand, each ply a different color, achieves a subtly muted or heathered effect (see figures C-15 and C-16). Texture can be obtained by employing threads of various weights, densities, shades, and forms (see the monkey pillow in figure C-12). An actual stitched tweed pattern is accomplished by alternating rows of colors (see the tweed pillow in figure C-14). The introduction of small, balanced areas of new colors, shading, and borders are additional means of creating variations. An unofficial trademark can become synonymous with your style. Inclusion of the same small design on each piece of your work will immediately designate the work as yours (see the change purse in figure S-15 and the friends pillow in figure C-20). This can be difficult if the selected design does not blend well with the total composition; but, done on a small scale, it should not interfere. Work it into a corner or along an edge. You don't have to use background colors: a distinctive new color that harmonizes can catch the eye without interfering with the whole composition. One of the colors in the main design is also very effective.

Sign your work with your name, signature, logo, or initials; a date is also appropriate. The craftsman's signature may be placed in the background on an edge or corner (see figure C-8) or elsewhere as a means of balance (see figure C-16). The signature is most pleasing when done in background colors; it can be encased in a stitched frame. The signature can also become an integral part of the central design (see the herringbone poppy pillow in figure C-12).

The recipient's monogram can be a handsome central theme or be placed inside a section of the focal design (see figure C-2 and the scissors case in figure C-20). An initial can be used effectively as a background or as part of the foreground (see the shoulderbag in figure C-12). Small, interspersed symbols or designs can illustrate the interests of the person to whom you are presenting the work. They show thought and consideration (see figure C-2) and will flatter the person who receives the gift as well as the person who created it.

Borders should coordinate with the design in the foreground as well as with the background (see figure C-19). They must never overpower either of them and should be compatible in color, style, and scale. Count your border stitches so that they will be equal and parallel on opposite sides. Do not estimate: count carefully. You can work from the ends of each side and fill in the center with a modification of the border design. This can be done deliberately or if the count does not permit the ends to meet perfectly midway. A corner pattern can be designed to connect the two if corners do not meet. In any case all corners must coordinate. The top and the bottom of the border must be as high as its sides are wide.

Additional finishing touches that can add special effects are tassels, fringes, turkey stitches, or ruffles. Welting can be done in a second color selected from the design (see figure C-5). Various types of cording such as monk's rope can also be used for an unusual trim (see "How to Select Patterned Backgrounds" for details).

Do not incorporate all these suggestions for individualizing into one canvas: the effect would be busy, confused, and overworked. Select one, two, or three techniques that you believe will best complement your work. Now that you have become aware of these many possibilities, you have only to design your own canvas. Select a central design and a background, purchase the basic tools, and you will have become a designer in your own right. Create!

OTHER MATERIALS

The suggestions mentioned for individualizing kits apply equally to those of you who are working from scratch with your own materials. Designing your own motifs and backgrounds is challenging, creative, and intriguing. The process can be facilitated by assembling the following equipment:

1. Graph paper is available in 8½" x 11" (21.59 x 27.94 cm) sheets or pads and in larger sizes such as 18" x 24" (45.72 x 60.96 cm). Graph paper that has been subdivided into sections such as eight or ten squares to the inch (2.54 cm) facilitates counting boxes while designing. An alternate to graph paper is canvas photostated with a different color backing.

2. Masking tape should be used on all edges except the selvage. Taping interlocking canvas will protect you and your clothes as well as the yarn and the canvas itself.

3. A drawing board can be made of tempered hardboard or plywood. Tape rather than tacks must be used on the lighter hardboard.

4. Stainless steel tacks prevent rusting.

5. Pencils are used on graph paper.

6. Colored pencils are used on graph paper, *never* on canvas. They are preferable to felt-tip markers because the colors can be erased.

7. Canvas comes in two basic types: mono and penelope. (Rug canvas is a variation of penelope.) The sizes indicate the number of meshes per inch (centimeter). Petit point and half-cross stitch as well as some other stitches require penelope. Check canvas for flaws such as knots, weak threads, or slubs. Measure the canvas to be sure that the gauge is correct. Polished canvas is higher in quality, wears better, and will not split as easily. Interlocking and plastic canvases are also available.

8. Tracing paper is available in sheets and pads of different sizes. Because it is transparent and nonporous, you can trace the design onto the canvas without marking the original drawing. Transparent acetate can be wiped off and reused; it is available at art-supply stores. Graphed tracing paper is available through architects' suppliers.

9. Waxed paper can be placed between graph paper and canvas to protect the original drawing.

10. Acrylic paint or indelible markers should be tested for colorfastness in water regardless of claims. Clear acrylic fixative can be sprayed lightly over the painted canvas for insurance. Too much might cause the paint to bleed. Oil paint dries very slowly; acrylics can be stitched within hours.

11. Acrylic polymer extends acrylic paint without affecting its waterproof quality.

12. White acrylic paint covers most errors made on white canvas. It is also useful in obtaining tints of various hues.

13. Paintbrushes need not be expensive: costly brushes wear poorly on canvas. Select brushes that do not have loose bristles. A fine, pointed, narrow brush; a medium brush; and a wide, blunt-edged brush will give you all the versatility you need.

14. Transparent tape with a matte finish permits the designer to work over taped areas of the graph paper without obstructing the lines.

15. Stain repellent is optional. Apply according to directions.

16. A magnifying glass is optional. The type that hangs from your neck is portable and permits free use of both hands. Table models are available with lights.

17. Good lighting is essential.

18. Yarn is available in many natural and synthetic materials, textures, and thicknesses. Cotton, linen, silk, metallic, nylon-velvet, and wool threads all provide different effects. Wool is the basic medium; Persian yarn is most suitable because it is adaptable to every type of needlepoint canvas. Each strand consists of three plies, and each ply contains two threads. It can be stripped down to fit the smallest gauge or accommodate #10 or #12 canvas without adding to its thickness—use rug yarn on rug canvas to fill larger gauges. Paternayan yarn has the best quality and sheen, and it offers the widest color range (343 colors).

19. Needles must have blunt tips. Tapestry needles are the type to use.

20. An open-ended thimble is the best type for those of you who use this accessory.

21. Scissors, both embroidery and shears, are essential. Embroidery scissors are used to clip stitches and yarn ends; shears, to cut canvas and yarn that is used in several thicknesses.

22. Tweezers are optional. They can be used to remove cut stitches.

23. A seam ripper or stitch remover is another option.

24. A frame is helpful in equalizing stitch tension and in reducing the amount of blocking required.

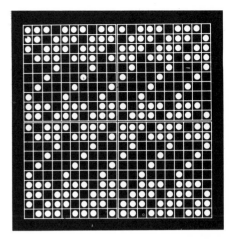

HOW TO SELECT PATTERNED BACKGROUDS

Experimentation and elimination will help you select your patterned background design. Choose a design appropriate to your degree of ability and to the central motif: it must be neither too powerful nor too weak. Complex or uncommon centers require basic backgrounds; easily recognizable forms can accommodate more detail in the background. The background should also blend with the style and theme of your central figure. If you like a particular background pattern that does not fit the focal design, try to adapt it. Work with the background's pattern and field: they can be reversed; the ratio between them can be altered to fit your requirements. The design's direction and size can also be changed to meet your needs. Two or more patterns may be combined to achieve the desired effect.

There are several ways to determine whether a background works with a foreground: superimpose the central design on the background design; hold it next to the background design; work a few background repeats (in graphed or stitched form) around it. Squint when you view the illustrations in order to get the full impact of the background's form.

A background pattern with an even-numbered repeat works best with an even-numbered central design; an odd-numbered pattern with an odd-numbered center. The same holds true for a center design with an odd or even number of geometric focal points. Place a mirror at a right angle to the paper; move it to reflect more than one repeat. Each background design should be duplicated in each direction in order to determine which is most pleasing. Turning the mirror at different angles shows the effect of varying the spacing between the repeats. The reflection also allows you to see the reverse or mirror image.

Backgrounds can be arranged on the canvas in one of two ways: at random or symmetrically. At random they appear as asymmetrical, uncentered running patterns or designs; they may not have a total repeat along the periphery. Symmetrical backgrounds can be seen as entities in themselves or as centered and completed repeats.

A patterned background and its central figure must support one another. They must be harmonious, with neither overpowering. Patterned backgrounds work best if the focal design does not have too many small lines or openings, which cause distraction and confusion. The pattern and the field of the background design should be in proper proportion to each other. A pleasing repeat along the periphery of the project is essential. Complex backgrounds can be combined with central designs that are easily recognizable; basic backgrounds do not interfere with intricate or highly stylized focal designs. The foreground and the background patterns should comprise a composition of harmony and balance, combining to form an artful entity.

Different stitches can reinforce the shape of a particular area of the design: a mosaic or scotch stitch, for example, will emphasize a square; a half-scotch stitch will enhance a triangle (see the monkey pillow in figure C-12). A background pattern will emerge if stitches such as these are done in two colors. The shape of the central design can be echoed in the form of the object itself (see the triangle pillow in figure C-12). Crewelpoint can give texture as well as a third dimension to a design; french knots can be used for eyes or flower centers. Small areas that require delicate work can be stitched in petit point if you are using penelope canvas (see the flower centers in figure C-16).

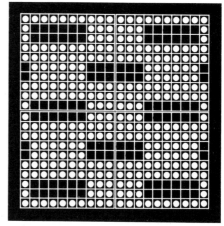

Further apart.

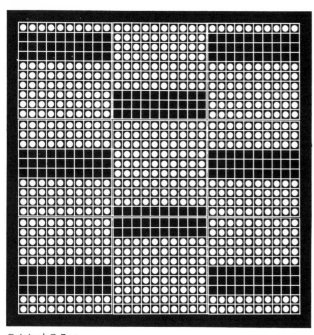

Original G-7.

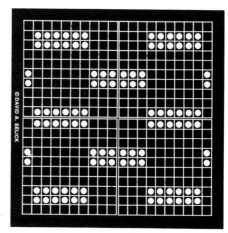

Pattern and field reversed.

Proportions changed.

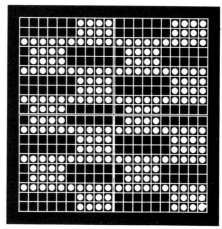

Closer together.

Any given pattern can be altered in a number of ways.

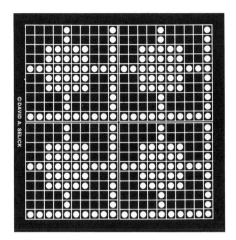

HOW TO CHOOSE COLORS

Selection of color is one of the most creative aspects of needlepoint, second only to the design. It controls the impact of the pattern and presents an opportunity for greater self-expression. Volumes have been written about color. We shall discuss it only as it applies to patterned backgrounds on canvas.

A color or combination of colors creates a focal point, a mood, and a style. Possible effects range from exotic to traditional, from serenity to action. The background pattern and the focal design should always complement each other. They should never compete but rather harmonize in style, color, and proportion.

Plan the entire color scheme at the beginning of the project and keep it simple. Check the colors together before starting to stitch. Look at them in the setting in which the finished project will be placed. View them in daylight and in artificial light. Check your yarn colors in daylight to ensure that they are from the same dye lot as others of matching hue. Do not place them against the canvas: check background and foreground colors against each other. This creates the same effect as that of the finished project.

You may decide that a particular color should be changed as you see the composition take form. Be flexible; do not hesitate to make a change in your original plan if it is necessary. Symmetrical center designs require greater attention to counting and afford no freedom for changes in color or stitch (see the triangle pillow in figure C-12 and figure C-13). Work a small amount of each color to see how it relates to the others before starting the actual canvas.

Stitched yarn will appear darker and less brilliant than it appears in the skein. Use a section on another piece of canvas or preferably along the margin as a test area for scale, color, and design. Limit the colors in your early canvases and gradually add more as you proceed to future works. Do not restrict yourself solely to the colors already used within a room: use them to extend the color range.

Colors can be combined in monochromatic, analogous, or complementary groups. Monochromatic color schemes are derived from the same hue but can vary widely in value and intensity. Analogous groupings have one color in common, such as blue, violet, and green, all of which contain blue. Complementary color pairs include red-green, yellow-violet, and blue-orange. They work best if one is major and the other supportive. Whenever one color is substituted for another, it gives a different feeling to the entire work (see figure C-13). Hues change in relation to neighboring colors and to the size of adjoining areas. Colors that are next to each other should never be too close in tone: they will blend together.

Bright colors are very effective when used properly. They bring the design forward and should be less intense as the design recedes. Bland hues reflect more pronounced ones. Colors that are close in hue and intensity can be separated or defined by a border or outline of a black substitute or white. They can be used to separate any two adjacent colors on the canvas. The black alternate is the darkest shade of the color used. Black is difficult to stitch. Its substitute makes the neighboring colors appear softer in tone and larger in area; white makes the adjacent colors darker and more brilliant. If the intensities are equally clear, neither will dominate; the result is an effect of vibration, as seen in many op-art works.

Shading should be done in dark tones of the original hue: use the darkest color available as a black substitute if you desire but *never* use black. Color tones are easier to work with and create softer impact. A light source behind you will show you where the shadows fall. They always must be constant, so your light source, real or imaginary, must be consistent. Highlighting is another form of shading that is worked in a similar manner (see the scissors case in figure C-20 and the Chinese-symbol cushion in figure C-14). Both methods give dimension to your work. Extra room should always be allowed for shadows or highlights: make the original design or letters smaller if necessary to prevent them from butting against one another. Designs on a large field need not be made smaller for shadowing: the background can be used as long as sufficient space is allowed for its repeats. Both highlights and shadows can be worked into the central design to provide a three-dimensional effect (see figure C-17, the herringbone poppy pillow in figure C-12, and figures C-15, C-16, and C-24).

A bold central design that is not readily familiar may require a background composed of two shades of the same color to clarify the pattern (see figures C-13 and C-21). The design appears more dominant and dynamic if close colors are used. Complex focal designs require simple backgrounds done in close, subtle colors (see figure C-8). A central design with a conventional theme can take bold background colors, since the viewer need not examine the central object to see what it is (see figure C-24 and the herringbone-poppy pillow in figure C-12). Bolder hues attract the eye: placement of such colors should be specific and controlled.

Use striking colors for simple stitches. Intricate stitches lose their detail if done in dark colors: lighter colors create their own highlights and shadows, allowing the interplay of threads to be seen. Long, flat stitches permit the color of the yarn to remain truest to its appearance in the skein. Crewelpoint is most effective if done in closely aligned tints and in shades of bright colors. Outlines in contrasting colors define shapes.

Color combinations create impact. Decide on a dramatic or subtle combination. Decisive impact makes a bold statement and demands attention, so definitive color should be employed (see figure C-5). Conversely, softness and elegance are achieved by using muted backgrounds in which the theme is gently carried out in form and color (see figures C-11 and C-19). Using each color in conjunction with its tints and shades accomplishes subtle changes. A mixture of yarn plies will produce tweeds as well as new shades and tints with subtle variations. Each approach must be developed with caution: the direct method should not become shocking; nor the subtle method, too bland.

Balance light and dark colors in the total design. One color should predominate; another may be second in importance. An accent color can be used effectively to highlight a detail, establish a focal point, or perk up a design if it is used judiciously (see the collar in figure C-1, the flower center in the herringbone-poppy pillow in figure C-12, and the dark green area in figure C-19). A small area of color can be picked up and repeated sparingly on the canvas for added balance. Many colors should not be used at once: they can make the canvas look jumbled, and the design can be lost. The overall effect—confusion. View the inverted work by squinting from a distance to check the balance of the composition.

Color is intriguing and boundless in its possibilities. Do not let it intimidate you. Good taste is no longer dictated: it is individual and eclectic. Almost anything that you find pleasing can be acceptable. Greater experimentation with color is permissible today than in the past. Artistic license extends beyond color to shape, size, and style. Utilize the intrinsic qualities of needlepoint to express your interpretation of the subject. Traditional color combinations are often discarded in favor of more daring and imaginative groupings. Unconventional color treatment of a given subject can be striking, creating a stylized effect. Experiment continually to gain experience in handling color; rely on your common color-sense.

HOW TO PREPARE, TRANSFER, AND STITCH THE PROJECT

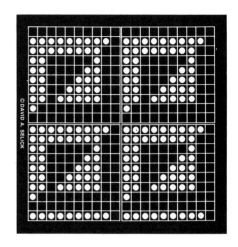

© DAVID A. SELICK

PREPARING THE PROJECT

Preparing the canvas for stitching requires careful organization. A well thought out plan permits you to preview the entire creation as it evolves step-by-step. Utilize the tools listed in "How to Choose Kits and Other Materials." The procedure is not difficult if you follow·this outline:

1. Select the subject, style, shape, size and colors.

  A. Consider the project's purpose and use.

  B. Coordinate the canvas size with the size of the central design.

    1. Intricate details require a small gauge.

    2. Avoid small openings in the central design.

    3. Use solid blocks of color.

  C. Balance the composition.

    1. Decide which element and color will predominate.

    2. Repeat shapes and colors.

    3. Make the central design a viable entity before adding background.

2. Locate and mark the center of the graph.

  A. Draw bisecting horizontal and vertical centerlines.

  B. Establish margins and extend the bisecting lines beyond the periphery.

3. Pencil the focal design in center of the graph paper.

  A. Mark the top of the design.

  B. Each box represents one thread intersection on the canvas.

  C. Allow a sufficient number of repeats along the background periphery.

  D. Square off curved lines.

  E. Fill in details.

  F. Color the central design.

  G. Check balance of the central drawing.

    1. Squint to see the total impression.

    2. Invert drawing and view a distance from final verification.

4. Place the selected background on the graph paper.

  A. Ascertain proportional harmony of background and the foreground.

  B. Check stylistic harmony of foreground and the background.

  C. Continue pattern count behind the central design (see figure C-4).

    1. Count carefully.

    2. Fill in spaces in the central design.

    3. The background mesh count between the central portions must be exact to ensure pattern continuity.

    4. Continue to the edge of the central design.

    5. Color the background.

TRANSFERRING THE PROJECT

To transfer the composition to the canvas, follow this procedure:

1. Prepare the canvas.

  A. Cut the canvas approximately 2" (5.08 cm) beyond the margins.

  B. Allow four rows for each seam.

C. Tape the edges.

D. Place the selvage on the side.

E. Mark the canvas at top and center.

2. Duplicate the design on the canvas.

A. Place the outline of the central design in the middle.

1. Count boxes out from the center.

2. Use indelible colors.

B. Color in details.

1. Carefully camouflage grid intersections with color.

a. Paint and yarn color should match.

b. Putty colors can be used.

2. Eradicate errors.

a. Use white acrylic paint.

b. Open clogged holes with an unthreaded needle.

C. Allow the paint to dry thoroughly before stitching.

3. Stitch the central design outward from the midpoint.

Each background consists of a pattern on a field. Either the pattern or the field must be chosen as the starting point for drawing and stitching the background. If the design is to be centered, one of the forms, either the pattern or the field, should be aligned midpoint to midpoint with the central design. Once the circles or squares are drawn or stitched onto the canvas, the alternate shape can be filled in automatically by working the open background areas. If the design is to be asymmetrical, you can begin in any area of your choice. Several methods can be used to transfer the background onto the canvas:

1. Painting the background is best. It camouflages any thread that might not be fully covered by yarn. Although it is time-consuming, it facilitates stitching.

2. The horizontal and vertical repeat of the background can be stitched from the graph and then used as a guide for the remainder. This is advisable only if the yarn is to cover the intersections of the grids completely, allowing no canvas to show.

3. Scoring the canvas is another method. Draw horizontal and vertical lines every ten rows, as in the graph. The repeats can be seen as one or two stitches more or less than the section of ten designated boxes, as shown on the graphs. A

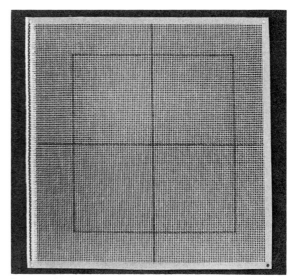

Prepare the canvas.

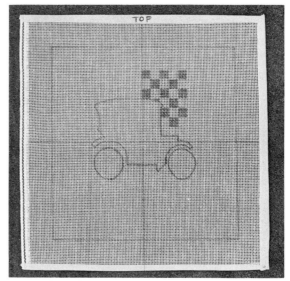

Duplicate the design on the canvas.

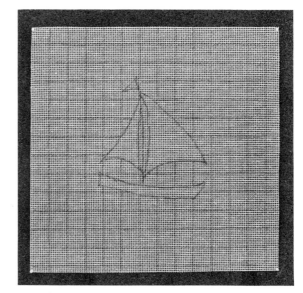

Score the canvas.

rhythm of stitching a particular design will emerge.

The repeat must be continued around and in the openings of the central design (see figure C-4). Assume that the focal design is gold and that the background is orange and brown. Spaces for the orange and brown pattern and field must be counted and allowed for behind the gold of the central design. The background must continue on either side as if there were no foreground in order to align with the other portions of the background.

The pattern can be seen as a design within a design: for example, a square in the center of a windowpane design bordered by a band (see figure C-16). This pattern can also be seen as a number of vertical and horizontal rows, each consisting of a specific number of stitches. These small inner patterns can help you to reproduce the repeat.

STITCHING THE PROJECT

The background can now be stitched on the canvas. If the entire background has not been meticulously painted on the canvas, follow the score marks, duplicate the horizontal and vertical repeats, or work directly from the graph.

1. Stitch the background repeats outward from the top center.
2. Stitch the background repeats down each side.
3. Draw the bottom repeats to ensure the correct count.
4. Fill in the remainder of the background, working outward from the center.
5. Accuracy can be assured by stitching either the entire pattern or the entire field (the circles or the squares) first.
6. Once that portion of the background is stitched, you can fill in the remainder.
7. Stop and count as you stitch in order to avoid mistakes that will throw off the exact repeat of the design.
8. Certain background shapes suggest particular stitches. Scotch or mosaic stitches emphasize squares or triangles (see figures S-13 and S-14, and the monkey pillow in figure C-12).
9. When you stitch, add four extra rows on each side for seams.
10. Any omissions can be detected in the finished canvas by holding the work in front of a light. Scrutinize it carefully.

The designs in *Patterned Backgrounds for Needlepoint* can be used in several ways: they can be used as backgrounds; their impact alone can create a canvas; two or more designs can be combined to form new geometric patterns. Change of scale, proportion, spacing, or angle of repeat creates variations. Pattern and field reversals provide a further option. Geometric designs are exciting possibilities.

Remember the limitations of the medium. Stitches can go in only one direction. Arched lines may appear asymmetrical. A vertical line moving from upper left to lower right produces a staggered, broken effect; a line moving from upper right to lower left yields a straight line.

Keep a photostated copy of the design on hand, indicating the colors and the stitches to be used. It serves as a portable reference for design as well as for color. A large or intricate canvas welcomes diversion. A second project with a dissimilar color scheme, size, scale, or style offers a change of pace. Work with a good light and stop designing or stitching before you tire. Most mistakes occur when working conditions are not suitable and when the needleworker is fatigued.

You are now aware of this fresh approach to needlepoint. Follow this concept as it best applies to your own ideas. In all instances the richness of the background will best enhance the canvas if it does not conflict with the central figure. The central and background designs should never overshadow one another: the purpose of the background is to enrich and reinforce the motif. A patterned background is necessary to a total concept, an integral composition.

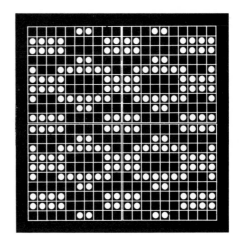

IDEAS AND PROJECTS

Ideas are everywhere. Project designs can be found in fabric, tile, wallpaper, rugs, and furniture shapes. Nature abounds with suggestions. Professional artists' works, children's drawings (see figures C-3 and C-21, and the target in figure C-22), greeting cards, chinaware, silhouettes, stained glass, and coloring books can be added to your references. Portions of complex pictures can be separated into individual entities by placing your hands thumb to thumb and index finger to index finger to form a frame.

Magazine clippings, sketches, and written descriptions should be kept in a folder. File them by category if you wish. Keep some graph paper handy for sketching; keep a pad on hand for recording ideas.

Stitched articles that will be exposed to soil can be sprayed. Lucite holders protect your handwork and give it outer support. Projects that will take a lot of wear require small stitches, preferably not vertical ones. Long, slanted or vertical stitches form loops that can snag and catch easily and do not wear well.

Many projects are listed below, arranged according to category. Many could be listed under several but are placed in the most obvious classification. Check each group carefully to discover the multitudinous possibilities. Let your imagination roam freely in search of designs and projects.

1. Animals: cage cover, collar, leash, sweater
2. Children: animal-shaped blocks, bookmark, doll-shaped pillow, earmuffs, child's mobile, patch, pencil holder, school banner, schoolbag

3. Clothes: bags (envelope, evening, shoulder, tote), belt, buckle, change purse, collar and trim, cuffs and trim, cummerbund, hat, hatband, pocket and trim, sandal straps, slippers, suspenders, tabard, tie, vest
4. Covers: address book, book cover with handles, card-table cover, checkbook, diary, memo pad, passport case, prayer book, stationery case, telephone book
5. Family: birth announcement, community map, family crest, family tree, graduation record, map of family locations, map of family origins, map of family travels, picture of home, school crest, wedding announcement
6. Games, hobbies, and interests: backgammon board, bicycle-seat cover, bowling-ball bag, chess- and checkerboard, coin and stamp replicas, collections (cars, guns, and andirons), golf-club socks, map, maze, racket cover (badminton, tennis), tennis bag, tic-tac-toe board, typewriter cover, vocational and avocational symbols
7. Holders: attaché case, bill file, briefcase, business card, canteen, cigarette box, cigarette case, clipboard top, credit-card case, flashlight case, handkerchief case, hosiery case, jewelry case, tobacco pouch, wallet
8. Home: bathroom: tissue-box cover, toilet-paper cover
   bedroom: bolster, headboard, pillow cover
   kitchen and dining room: canister covers, napkin holder, napkin rings, placemats, recipe file, teapot cozy, toaster cover, trivet
   living room: card-table cover, chair seat, desk accessories, fire screen, ice bucket, piano bench

general: armrest, backrest, bellpull, book-ends, door sign, door stop, drapery tie-backs, footstool, hand plate for door or light switch, lamp base or shade, magazine rack, mail tray, mirror frame, picture frame, room partition, rug (game, regular), screen, panels, stair runner or treads, wallhanging, wastepaper basket, Turkish floor pillow, window seat

9. Jewelry: barette, bracelet, choker, cufflinks, headband, pendant, tie bar, watchband

10. Notions: buttons, calendar, coasters, compact case, comb and brush case, contact lens case, cosmetic case, elbow patches, eyeglass case, fabric flowerpot band, hatstand, key case or tag, lighter case, lipstick case, luggage tag, manicure-set case, pincushion, pillbox, sachet case, scissors case, shoebag

11. Miscellaneous: car seat, clock face or frame, holiday decorations, luggage-rack straps, motto, paperweight, pew cushion, portrait, religious altar or ark curtains, reproductions of art (juvenile, professional, sculpture), sampler

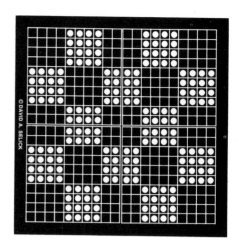

LIST OF SOURCES

The following firms sell to the trade only. Your local needlepoint shops can obtain their products for you.

1. Paternayan Brothers, Inc. (canvas and wool)
   312 East 95 Street
   New York, N.Y. 10028
2. Plex-Art Designs (lucite products)
   80 Bergen Turnpike
   Little Ferry, N.J. 07643
3. Eberhard Faber, Inc. (Needlecraft® markers and pens)
   Crestwood
   Wilkes-Barre, Pa. 18703
4. Needlepoint Technology (tapestry tabulator)
   P.O. Box 11
   Towaco, N.J. 07082
5. Needle-ease (frames)
   81 Uplands Drive
   West Hartford, Conn. 06107

INDEX OF GRAPH ILLUSTRATIONS

INDEX

Italics refer to name of design.

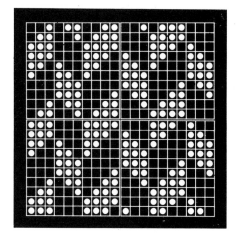